D0942222

The Diary of Laura

THE DIARY OF Laura

PERSPECTIVES ON A REGGIO EMILIA DIARY

Edited by Carolyn Edwards and Carlina Rinaldi

in Collaboration with Reggio Children

Redleaf Press®
www.redleafpress.org
800-423-8309

Published by Redleaf Press
10 Yorkton Court
St. Paul, MN 55117 USA
www.redleafpress.org

© 2009 by Carolyn Edwards, the Municipality of Reggio Emilia-Istituzione Preschools and Infant-Toddler Centers, and Reggio Children S.r.l.

All rights reserved. Unless otherwise noted on a specific page, no portion of this publication may be reproduced or transmitted in any form or by any means, electronic or mechanical, including photocopying, recording, or capturing on any information storage and retrieval system, without permission in writing from the publisher, except by a reviewer, who may quote brief passages in a critical article or review to be printed in a magazine or newspaper or electronically transmitted on radio, television, or the Internet.

The translation of the diary is an authorized translation of the publication originally published in Italian in 1983 by the Municipality of Reggio Emilia, Italy, under the title *Il diario al nido per fermare la storia dei bambini: Storia di Laura*.

International center for the defense and promotion of the rights and potential of all children
Reggio Emilia, Italy. All rights reserved.

Reggio Children S.r.l.
Via Bligny, 1/a - C.P. 91 Succursale 2
42100 Reggio Emilia, Italy
www.reggiochildren.it
First edition 2009
Jacket design by Brad Norr Design
Interior typeset in Fairfield and designed by Jim Handrigan
See page 139 for jacket and interior photo credits.
Printed in Canada
18 17 16 15 14 13 12 11   2 3 4 5 6 7 8 9

Library of Congress Cataloging-in-Publication Data
Il diario al nido per fermare la storia dei bambini : Storia di Laura. English
  The diary of Laura : perspectives on a Reggio Emilia Diary / edited by Carolyn Edwards and Carlina Rinaldi. — 1st ed.
    p. cm.
  Translation of: Il diario al nido per fermare la storia dei bambini : Storia di Laura.
  Includes bibliographical references.
  ISBN 978-1-933653-52-5 (alk. paper)
  1. Reggio Emilia approach (Early childhood education) 2. Education, Preschool—Italy—Reggio Emilia.   I. Edwards, Carolyn P. II. Rinaldi, Carlina.
III. Title.
LB1029.R35D5213 2008
372.210945'43—dc22
                              2008002121

               ISBN 978-1-60554-152-5 (paperback)

*To Laura
and all
the children*

THE DIARY OF LAURA

Acknowledgments | ix

Introduction | Setting the Scene | 1
Carolyn Edwards

PART ONE: REINVENTING LAURA

Reinventing Laura | An Educational Diary in a Reggio Emilia Nido | 9
Carlina Rinaldi (translated by Silvia Betta)

Arcobaleno Infant-Toddler Center Floor Plan | 16

PART TWO: STORY OF LAURA

The Diary at the Infant-Toddler Center to Record Stories of Children | *Story of Laura* | 21
(translated by Silvia Betta)

PART THREE: A REUNION AT ARCOBALENO

An Encounter with Laura | 57
Eluccia, Giuliana, Paola, and Tiziana Meet Laura, Davide, and Filomena
Laura and the Diary | 62
Giuliana Campani, Paola Cavazzoni, Eluccia Forghieri, and Tiziana Bini (translated by Silvia Betta)

PART FOUR: REFLECTIONS FROM AROUND THE WORLD

How the Infant Teacher's Context Influences the Content of Diaries | 67
J. Ronald Lally

In the Footsteps of Laura's Teachers | A Scottish Perspective | 77
Pat Wharton

Laura's Diary | An Australian Perspective | 85
Jan Millikan

Contextualizing the Watch Episode of Laura | Its Significance to Korean Educators | 97
Moonja Oh

"Tell Laura I Love Her, Tell Laura I Need Her" | A Swedish Song | 107
Harold Göthson

Final Reflections | *The Diary of Laura* as a Tool for Professional Development | 123
Carolyn Edwards

ACKNOWLEDGMENTS

We wish to thank all of the children, parents, educators, and colleagues who have been part of the system of infant-toddler centers and preschools in Reggio Emilia and whose educational stories contributed to the development of our way of compiling educational diaries. We particularly wish to acknowledge the children, parents, teachers, and staff at Asilo Nido Arcobaleno whose images grace the pages of this book. We are also deeply appreciative of the support of Reggio Children in creating this volume, especially for the devoted help of Annamaria Mucchi. We received additional support and resources from the University of Nebraska–Lincoln, and are deeply indebted to our translator, Silvia Betta, for her dedication to the project. Certainly our colleagues who contributed essays deserve a large share of credit for the rich content within this volume, and we also wish to thank participants at many conferences in the United States and Canada who attended sessions at which Laura's story was presented, accompanied by reflective questions that seemed to inspire intense and stirring discussions. We appreciate the concern and care with which Redleaf Press has approached the editing and production of this book. Finally, we wish to thank all of our colleagues in Italy and around the world whose intellectual friendship has meant so much to us and to our personal and professional growth.

Introduction

SETTING THE SCENE

Carolyn Edwards
University of Nebraska–Lincoln
USA

WHAT IS AN INFANT EDUCATIONAL DIARY?
FOR WHOM IS IT CREATED?
WHAT KIND OF STORIES DOES IT TELL?
WHAT QUESTIONS DOES IT RAISE ABOUT QUALITY IN EARLY
CHILDHOOD CARE AND EDUCATION?
AND HOW DID THE PRACTICE COME ABOUT IN REGGIO EMILIA?

This volume has at its heart a new edition of a small book published by the Municipality of Reggio Emilia in 1983 that represented a milestone in the experience of Reggio Emilia educators and stated many principles of their educational philosophy. I first became acquainted with the original *Storia di Laura* (*Story of Laura*) when Lella Gandini took me to Reggio Emilia in the spring of 1983, but it was not until many years later that its full significance and potential for use as a tool for promoting professional development of early childhood educators emerged. It is a pleasure to be able to collaborate with Carlina Rinaldi and Reggio Children to offer this gift of Laura's diary, surrounded by explanations of how the educational diary evolved as a strategy of practice in Reggio Emilia, reflections by experts from around the world who have a deep acquaintance with the infant-toddler centers and preschools of Reggio Emilia, and most surprising of all, images of Laura now grown up, with her infant son and her mother, in reunion with some of her original teachers, who kindly share their own reflections.

The early 1980s were a time of ferment and change in Reggio Emilia and of expansion for the infant-toddler component of the public early childhood system serving children from birth to age six (Edwards, Gandini, and Forman 1998; Gandini and Edwards 2001). Infant-toddler centers were somewhat new. Reggio families were concerned about whether center-based care was good for infants and toddlers and what the separation might mean for them and their families. Could children so young adjust to a children's center? How would that adjustment influence them and their relationships to their parents? How could parents and teachers "share" a baby? As Carlina Rinaldi describes in her original 1983 introduction to *Story of Laura*, as pedagogical coordinator she worked closely with the teachers of Arcobaleno

From left: Vea Vecchi, Carolyn Edwards, Loris Malaguzzi, and Lella Gandini, in front of the exhibit "The Eye, If It Jumps Over the Wall" in Reggio Emilia, 1983.

("Rainbow") Infant-Toddler Center to conduct a study, that is, teacher action research, on the process of the infant's adjustment to the center. (Note: The Italian term for infant-toddler center is *asilo nido*, or "safe nest," and *nido* literally means "nest" in Italian and is the term used for the public infant-toddler centers of Reggio Emilia.) The city published this as a part of Quaderni Reggiani, a series of publications intended to speak openly to the city about the new services for children under three years old that the public administration was offering. Other booklets in the Quaderni Reggiani series addressed such topics as play, naps and sleep, and use of puppets at the infant-toddler centers.

Loris Malaguzzi, founder and director of the Reggio Emilia system of public preschools and infant-toddler centers, received Lella Gandini and me in 1983 and gave us a tour of several preschool centers and of an exhibit, later to be called "The Hundred Languages of Children" (Reggio Children 1996). In the afternoon we visited Arcobaleno, and our photos show Ivetta Fornaciari and another teacher working during the children's naptime on the diaries that would soon be given to the graduating families as parting gifts. This same photo reveals Loris Malaguzzi inspecting a diary with a curly-haired toddler who had awoken early from his nap. It reveals not only Loris's consummate ease and delight with children but also his intense absorption in all of the small details of the daily life in the centers. At the time, I was a young parent of two small children and beginning my early childhood education career, and I was enchanted and intrigued by what I saw at Arcobaleno.

Loris Malaguzzi inspecting one of the diaries, 1983.

By the time I rediscovered Laura's diary more than twenty years later, however, I was able to bring much more depth of experience and knowledge to its appreciation and interpretation. Silvia Betta, a doctoral student in bilingual education at the University of Nebraska, has translated Laura's diary and the other Italian pieces of this volume into

English. Silvia is an ideal translator because she combines native Italian language with knowledge of educational theory and philosophy. She is also the mother of four children, so *Story of Laura* connects with her both intellectually and personally. Indeed, Laura's diary turns out to connect with many educators in a powerful way, no matter what age group they teach, and it suggests new ways to use pedagogical documentation in early childhood programs and teacher education and to promote a family-centered, relationship-based approach to services for very young children and their families.

From the threads woven together to create this book, readers will construct their own interpretations of what it means for them and their work. Carlina Rinaldi opens the book with a history of how the educational diary emerged as a form of pedagogical documentation, and thus her essay provides the context for the original story as well as a glimpse into the creative forces at work in the early years in Reggio Emilia and still alive today (Rinaldi 2006). This chapter is followed by *Story of Laura*, much like the original except now with the addition of text in English opposite the original Italian. Next comes the account of the reunion at Arcobaleno

(*Left*) A teacher and older toddlers look at a diary together, 1983.

The staff of the Arcobaleno Infant-Toddler Center, 1980s.

(*Right*) Loris Malaguzzi leading the way into Arcobaleno Infant-Toddler Center, 1983.

A teacher playing with infants, 1980s.

Infant-Toddler Center by Giuliana Campani, Paola Cavazzoni, Eluccia Forghieri, and Tiziana Bini, which details how Laura and her family remember their time at the center and how it affected them, as well as what the educators understood at the time and have come to understand in retrospect.

Finally, the reflective essays start what we hope will be a long and fruitful dialogue on what the diary means to educators today and how we can use it to inform our work. J. Ronald Lally from the United States suggests that infant-toddler teachers learn to observe as participant observers, in order to plan in a way that more deeply respects the children's interests. Pat Wharton from Scotland lays out ways *Story of Laura* can serve as one useful example as teachers seek concrete strategies for compiling an educational diary. Jan Millikan from Australia considers how to operate within the boundaries of one's own situation when adapting ideas from others—for example, when responding to the cultural diversity and part-time attendance patterns typical of her society. Moonja Oh from Korea calls on educators to use Laura's diary as an inspiration to break out of old assumptions and unproductive thought patterns that block our capacity to see the beauty of what is before us in everyday events of teaching and learning. Harold Göthson from Sweden extends that message as he describes the years in which the work of Reggio educators was intimidating to Swedish teachers until as a group they found their strength within themselves and their own national educational culture. Finally, I conclude with a summary intended to help teachers make connections to their own practices: a set of reflective questions I have used in workshops with teachers and students and some themes and guidelines that emerge from the reflective essays and move us forward toward what Loris Malaguzzi (1993) called an "education based on relationships."

Carolyn Edwards, EdD, is a Willa Cather Professor and a professor of psychology and child, youth, and family studies at the University of Nebraska–Lincoln. She is an internationally recognized expert on child development, early childhood education, cross-cultural studies, and teacher preparation. She is an author or editor of many books and articles, including Bambini: The Italian Approach to Infant/Toddler Care *(Teachers College Press, 2001);* The Hundred Languages of Children: The Reggio Emilia Approach, Advanced Reflections, 2nd ed. *(Ablex, 1998); and* The Hundred Languages of Children: The Reggio Emilia Approach to Early Childhood Education *(Ablex, 1993).*

Edwards, Carolyn, Lella Gandini, and George Forman, eds. 1998. *The hundred languages of children: The Reggio Emilia approach, advanced reflections.* 2nd ed. Greenwich, CT: Ablex.

Gandini, Lella, and Carolyn Edwards, eds. 2001. *Bambini: The Italian approach to infant/toddler care.* New York: Teachers College Press.

Malaguzzi, Loris. 1993. For an education based on relationships. *Young Children* 49 (1): 9–12.

Reggio Children. 1996. *The hundred languages of children: Narrative of the possible. Proposals and intuitions of children from the infant-toddler centers and preschools of the city of Reggio Emilia.* Catalog of the exhibit *The hundred languages of children.* Municipality of Reggio Emilia Infant-Toddler Centers and Preschools. Reggio Emilia, Italy: Reggio Children.

Rinaldi, Carlina. 2006. *In dialogue with Reggio Emilia: Listening, researching and learning.* London and New York: Routledge.

Part One

REINVENTING LAURA

Reinventing Laura

An Educational Diary in a Reggio Emilia Nido

Carlina Rinaldi
Reggio Children
Reggio Emilia, Italy
(Translated by Silvia Betta)

It is sweet as well as demanding to reinvent Laura and her diary more than twenty years after our first encounter, our "growing together." Truly, Laura and we (the teachers and I) have in a sense existed and continue to exist partly because we "narrated ourselves," because we entrusted the narrative with the meaning and value of our being together. Certainly, in the words and images captured by the teachers there is not only Laura with her discoveries and conquests, but also the teachers themselves, with their knowledge, their wonders, and their values. Laura's diary is thus a biography, the biography of a relationship, or more precisely of more relationships.

In the text transpires the pleasure of narrating to understand, narrating to give existence and to exist. Through the organization of data and events, chosen for some relevance among all those that happened, the narrative becomes a form of thought and gives structure and meaning to a story, thus giving it existence, transforming it into a life story, recreating it and giving it new meaning. "There is no life if it is not told," said

Jerome Bruner, one of the most internationally renowned psychologists and longtime friend of our schools. The narrative gives meaning but also visibility to life, bringing synthesis, underscoring the salient features, the choices that give meaning to the past, a daily flow that would otherwise get lost in anonymity.

The diary and the concept itself of school documentation fall within and find meaning in this idea of narrative. After all, the diary has represented a structure and a phase that was vital to the elaboration of the concept of epistemological documentation as it was conceived in the Reggio Emilia experience. It was back in the early 1970s that Loris Malaguzzi suggested keeping a class diary. He suggested this to the teachers, who intuitively recognized its value; we later discovered its meaning and its implications on the planning and evaluation level.

The diaries were big striped notebooks, handwritten with a certain elegance and care to be readable and to be shared with colleagues. A new notebook was usually started at the beginning of each year; one notebook contained the story of one year. The first page normally listed the names of the children and the teachers. After that was a space to update or make any changes, which were all noted.

The narrative gives meaning but also visibility to life.

At the beginning the meaning of the diary was not very clear to anybody because when compiling the diary some teachers noted the events in chronological order (much like a logbook). Later, as teachers progressed in their use of the diary and realized its value, they shifted from the class diary to an individual diary for each child.

Furthermore, it became more and more evident that the diaries were used to record the teachers' thoughts and responses, such as their feelings of surprise at certain moments or their feelings of concern and not knowing exactly what to do at others. The notes were used by the teachers to plan and motivate activities, to make explicit the "whys," the reasons behind choices, the real or presumed motivations, and particularly the precise description of events. Once a week the diaries were exchanged among the teachers during the weekly professional development meeting, and the most important passages were read and discussed during department and school in-service meetings.

The diary contents were also shared with parents. In fact, several group meetings were (and still are) held each year with the families, with the first meeting held even before the school year began, to tell the parents what to expect and how they might help their child feel at ease in the center. At this first group meeting, the families were introduced to one another and began to build a sense of community and closeness by learning such things as where one another lived, how many other children they had, and what kind of work they did. Parents had a chance to share their feelings or concerns about the infant-toddler center, and they were told they could spend as much time with their child in the infant room as they wanted during the upcoming days. To help ease the process of separation, it was suggested that parents might tell their child they were leaving and step out of the room for a few moments, to begin to give their child the idea of the parents' leaving and returning. Parents were also encouraged to bring along other family members, such as a grandmother, who might be feeling worried about this new infant-toddler center experience. As the school year began, more parent meetings were held (several close to the beginning of the year, and then a few others as time went on, for perhaps six meetings a year in total). In those days, it was not so common for fathers to come to the center, and therefore a parent meeting was held just for fathers as a way of supporting them. The sharing of the teachers' notes and photographic slides at all of the parent meetings turned out to be important opportunities for families to reflect on all the issues and feelings they had in common and on what their children's experiences in the center had been.

As all of this work progressed, the need arose to make annotations, which sometimes had been written too implicitly and obscurely, clearer and more legible, more apt to be shared with readers who had not participated in the event. To capture events accurately, teachers often kept little notepads that they could pull out of their pockets and use to jot down quick notes that they could expand on later and write into the children's diaries. Such attempts to take quick "mental snapshots" sparked the idea of taking camera snapshots to preserve images of the important moments as they took place. This required increasing the teachers' understanding of photography and its appropriate and timely use, aimed at recording what was significant in the situation. And from the photography came the idea to include photos, drawings, and coauthored writings in each diary, in order to capture the diversity of possible perspectives around an event, thus encouraging comparison and discussion.

These are the first although not yet fully conscious signs of what will be an essential trait of documentation as we conceive it today, that is, a documentation that is able to offer a detailed description and that is at the same time rich with a diversity of visual and photographic images, as a testimony of the epistemological event pertaining to the child as well as the teacher.

Similarly, another turning point in the evolution of the "diary" was the decision to highlight (together with or instead of the daily events involving all children) the description and commentary of microepisodes, or microstories, that have and give continuity to individual experiences. Laura's diary develops from this tendency to use microstories to make evident the relationship between the individual story of each child and the story of the peer group. The peer group gives context to the individual story, and vice versa.

Children are rarely captured isolated and separated from one another but are most likely described within the ever-changing dynamics they develop with the teacher and the other children. Clearly, there is no such thing as a "given" child or a "given" context. And this type of documentation has a strong qualitative value that makes the diaries of particular interest today. The teachers' effort to not document the child in isolation but to also consider the context surrounding the child gives rise to a contextual documentation, describing the "where" and the "how," and also hypothesizing the "why." Russian psychologist Lev Vygotsky's and Swiss psychologist Jean Piaget's writings were at the time the most relevant readings, but anthropological readings were also pointing more and more to context definition and to a systemic view of education and pedagogy.

The writing of the diary (a form of documentation) was useful to the educator as practice in observation while watching the events that occurred and occur daily in the educational context under a "magnifying glass," events that would not have acquired meaning and value if not captured and written in the diary. The educational approach transpiring from those diaries is far distant from the concept of laboratory, that is, from an environment in which independent and dependent variables are isolated. The diaries were in this sense ecological, open to the constant change of conditions and to capturing situations in their richness and complexity. A precious element is the recurrent attention to describing teachers' subjective reactions to specific facts or lived experiences: The teacher feels like a part of the context. She is herself context and is an engaged and passionate participant of the context. The qualities of participant observation and biased narrative are evident, but so is the generosity of the narrative, rich in the emotions lived in the documentation and education. The documentation is in fact a process of "participation," as the teacher "is part," and thus participant, in the process. For this reason, the reflectiveness necessary when writing and possible when rereading (individually and in groups) is what transforms the anecdote into knowledge and the knowledge into collective and connecting knowing.

The teacher feels like a part of the context.

Teachers' professional development and class meetings with families provided the setting that ensured the diary would become a source of knowledge and an instrument for planning new opportunities. The diary became a structure essential to a progressive curriculum development, or to better planning. The discoveries of the child and a group were a shared joy, an opportunity to understand and plan new spaces and activities. The environments changed on the basis of those annotations, and the anecdote became a sign of a child or group learning process. The daily conversations with parents became richer, because both parents and teachers were more competent. The diary could be read every day and taken home, and sometimes parents themselves wrote annotations and comments.

Is the Form of Documentation Called "Diary" Still of Interest after Twenty Years?

I believe that the diary is a renewed instrument of possible and new efficacy, with the specifications, acquisitions, and awareness developed through all these years around the pedagogical (and epistemological) documentation, and with the difference that the media can bring to the narrated documentation (for example, videos, photos, recordings).

This is true particularly of the infant room. New technologies (computer, Internet, digital camera) allow the diary to maintain its quality of private writing, but also to become, almost at the same time, "public," a discussion forum opportunity for the teachers first, and then the parents (with no precise order, however).

A new opportunity for dialogue is thus created, although it needs to preserve the rhythms and times that are proper to the diary and set it apart from the daily correspondence of an e-mail. The time in the diary is a slower time: It is the time of reflectiveness, of pauses, and interior listening. It is the time of memory.

Memory is life, always evolving, vulnerable, susceptible to latency and reawakening: the annotations collected and organized during the day are by nature partial and thus open, awaiting comments, annotations, and suggestions from others.

I believe that the diary can still be a useful and important instrument for the development of new teachers, but also an effective instrument for continuing professional development.

Like Laura's diary, a diary can be an instrument of great value for the present and the future.

Carlina Rinaldi is president of Reggio Children and professor at the University of Modena and Reggio Emilia in Italy. From 1970 until his death in 1994, she worked side by side with Loris Malaguzzi in the municipal infant-toddler and preschool system of Reggio Emilia, where she was the first pedagogical coordinator. She lectures frequently on the Reggio Emilia experience, and has published many articles, chapters, and books in Italian and English, including "Organization as a Value," in Innovations in Early Education: The International Reggio Exchange 8, *no. 1 (Fall 2000); "The Image of the Child and the Child's Environment as a Fundamental Principle," in* Bambini: The Italian Approach to Infant/Toddler Care *(Teachers College Press, 2001); "The Teacher as Researcher," in* Innovations in Early Education: The International Reggio Exchange 10, *no. 2 (Spring 2003); "The Pedagogy of Listening: The Listening Perspective from Reggio Emilia," in* Innovations in Early Education: The International Reggio Exchange 8, *no. 4 (Fall 2001); and "The Relationships between Documentation and Assessment," in* Innovations in Early Education: The International Reggio Exchange 11, *no. 1 (Winter 2004). She is an editor and author of* Making Learning Visible: Children as Individual and Group Learners *(Harvard Project Zero and Reggio Children, 2001), and author of* In Dialogue with Reggio Emilia: Listening, Researching and Learning *(Routledge, 2006).*

ARCOBALENO INFANT-TODDLER CENTER

1

2

3

4

5

6

7

8

9

10

11

12

Floor Plan

ARCOBALENO INFANT-TODDLER CENTER

1 Entrance

5 Toddlers from 18 to 24 months

9 Toddlers from 10 to 18 months

2 Central "piazza"

6 Space for sound and music exploration

10 Bathroom – changing area

3 Dining area for toddlers from 18 to 36 months

7 Atelier

11 Infants

4 Toddlers from 24 to 36 months

8 Dining area for infants and small toddlers

12 Sleeping area – infants

Floor Plan

PHOTOS FROM THE 1980s

Part Two

STORY OF LAURA

Municipio di
Reggio Emilia

Assessorato
Pubblica Istruzione

Marzo 1983

**quaderni
reggiani**

il "diario„ al nido

per fermare la storia dei bambini

storia di Laura

THE DIARY

AT THE INFANT-TODDLER CENTER
TO RECORD STORIES OF CHILDREN

STORY OF
Laura

Reggio Emilia Department of Education,
March 1983

From the series Quaderni Reggiani

I

INTRODUZIONE

IL DIARIO COME STRUMENTO DI LAVORO

La parola "diario" assume significati diversi se condo l'ambito e le finalità che si pone: vi é il diario intimista, molto in voga nella letteratura romantica dell'ottocento e caro a molte adolescenti di ieri e di oggi, dove l'autore racconta sia i fatti della sua vita che gli effetti delle sue passioni e dei suoi ideali.

Accanto a questo, letterario, si é sviluppato un nuovo modo di concepire e realizzare il diario, determinato soprattutto dallo sviluppo di nuove scienze, quali ad esempio l'etologia: il diario osservativo, quello che si compila fissando con assoluta precisione il soggetto da osservare, registrandolo con sistematicità, (anche ogni giorno), metodicità e rigore.

Colui che scrive deve essere il più possibile fedele al fatto così com'é, sforzandosi di essere il più "obiettivo" possibile.

Il "diario al nido" si differenzia sostanzialmente da entrambi, pur conservando alcuni (pochi) tratti dell'uno e dell'altro; é soprattutto una raccolta di segni,

di momenti, di sequenze di gesti e di parole del bambino con l'adulto, con i bambini, con le cose: é un diario per appunti, un diario "schizzato" dall'operatore che annota, appena trova il tempo, sul block notes tascabile, un materiale breve, rapido, da integrare in seguito con la memoria. Nasce, questo materiale, da un patto convenzionale d'azione tra l'accadimento - il codice che lo segna, lo ferma - e il ricordo di chi ne é stato testimone e lo vuole rimettere nel cerchio del pensiero.

INTRODUCTION

THE DIARY AS A WORK TOOL

The word diary takes on different meanings based on its context and goals: in the introspective diary, very common during the 1800s in the romantic literature and dear to many adolescents of today and yesterday, the author recalls events from his or her own life and also the effects of his or her passions and ideals. In addition to this literary form, a new way to conceive and develop the diary came from the development of new sciences, such as ethology where the observational diary is compiled with participant observations written down with exact precision and entries are recorded systematically (even daily) with method and rigor. The writer has to be as faithful as possible to the events as they are, striving to be as objective as possible.

The diary at the infant-toddler center is substantially different from either one of these two forms, even though it retains some traits of both. It is mainly a collection of signs and moments, a series of gestures and words of the child with the adult, with the children, and with the objects. It is a diary of notes, a diary sketched by the educator, who quickly writes some material in a notebook as soon as possible, material that he or she will later fill in with the aid of memory. The material in the diary comes from an action agreement between the event, the code that records it, and the memory of the person who witnessed it and who now puts it back in his or her circle of thoughts.

II

La trascrizione cerca di cogliere non tanto "il bambino", ma l'evento, ciò che sta a mezza via tra il bambino e l'educatore, il bambino e i bambini, il bambino e le cose e gli spazi: anzi l'evento é nella relazione, nel contesto della relazione, provocato dalla stessa relazione tra i diversi soggetti.

Quello che "appunti" non é tutto del bambino, né dell'adulto, é nella dinamica che nasce dal loro rapporto, nel baricentro della relazione asimmetrica che lo garantisce.

Il codice utilizzato può essere quello scritto ma anche quello fotografico o la loro integrazione: la parola e l'immagine, integrandosi e alternandosi, possono completare lo "schizzo" soprattutto se vi é una sufficiente consapevolezza del mezzo fotografico in particolare e una sua finalizzazione corretta e tempestiva, tesa cioé a fermare ciò che c'é di significativo della situazione.

Le annotazioni vengono fatte nel corso dell'intero anno scolastico, ma l'intervallo di tempo tra un appunto e l'altro é irregolare: il diario non si fa sistematicamente, ma quando l'evento é considerato di nuova significatività, quando suscita, nei suoi protagonisti, sorpresa e probabile aggiunta di conoscenza e di problemi.

PER CHI IL DIARIO

Per gli operatori é certamente un modo di affinare le proprie capacità di cogliere i fatti laddove e quando accadono; per autoanalizzarsi e analizzare, assieme alle colleghe, il come e il perché degli eventi e dei comportamenti propri e dei bambini: per informare i genitori e insieme leggere e interpretare i "segni del bambino

The writing strives to capture not so much the child but the event that takes place between the child and the educator, the child and the children, the child and the objects and spaces. In addition, the event is in the relationship, is in the context of the relationship, and stems from the same relationship among the different subjects. Those notes are not all on the child, nor the adult, but on the dynamics that arise in their relationship, on the center of the asymmetrical relation that is at the basis of that relationship.

The code used can be the written code but also the photographic code or a mixture of both: the words and the images, together or alternated, can complete the sketch when there is a sufficient understanding of the particular photographic means and of its correct and appropriately timed use, aimed at recording that which is significant in the situation. The annotations are made during the entire school year, but the time lapse between one entry and the next one varies: the diary is not systematic but is compiled when the event is considered to have new significance, when it arouses surprise in its characters and is likely to increase knowledge and problems.

For Whom Is the Diary Created?

For the educators, it is certainly a way to refine their abilities to see the events when and where they happen, to analyze and self-reflect, together with colleagues, on the reasons and the modalities behind the events and behaviors, their own and those of the children; to inform the parents and to read together and interpret the "signs" of the child in the context of the experience.

III

nel contesto dell'esperienza".

<u>Per i genitori</u> un'occasione per riavvicinare il bam-
bino e reindagarlo attraverso l'occhio più distac
cato e talvolta più obiettivo o più osservativo
delle operatrici: per conoscere di più com'é il
bambino a distanza da loro e immerso in un' area
esistenziale diversa da quella familiare: per a-
prire nuovi varchi alla riflessione.

<u>Per il bambino</u> la consapevolezza,
avvertita anche attraverso u
na più alta comunicazione,at
tenzione e sensibilità dell-
l'ambiente che lo circonda,
di essere un "soggetto amoro
so"; una garanzia in più di
un intervento educativo per-
sonalizzato; un documento
che, diventato più grande,
gli consentirà di leggere al
cuni frammenti della sua sto
ria.

I "diari", qui   riportati,
tratti dal diario di Laura, si
susseguono in ordine temporale e
riferiscono gli accadimenti, le
mosse, i "passi", le scoperte,la
geografia e i sentimenti delle re
lazioni instaurate da Laura con
gli adulti, i coetanei, i giocat
toli, gli spazi interni ed ester

ni nei primi mesi di frequenza al nido.

For the parents, it is an opportunity to get closer to the child and to study him or her through the eyes of the educators, which are more detached and sometimes more objective and observant; to learn more about what the child is like while away from home, when immersed in an existential area different from the familiar one; and to open new avenues for reflection.

For the child, awareness is gained through a higher communication, attention, and sensitivity of the environment around him or her, and from being a "subject of love"; the diary documents a personalized educational intervention, a document that when he or she is grown up will enable him or her to read fragments of his or her own story.

The diaries reported here are excerpts from Laura's diary and are listed in their chronological order. They depict the events, the motions, the steps, the discoveries, the geography, and the feelings of the relationships developed by Laura with the adults, the classmates, the toys, the internal and external spaces during her first months at the infant-toddler center.

IL DIARIO AL NIDO
PER FERMARE LA STORIA DI OGNI BAMBINO

S T O R I A   D I   L A U R A

E' un esempio di come si possono
registrare le storie dei piccoli
con la penna e la macchina fotografica

CHI E' LAURA

Laura é nata il 13/10/1980, primogenita di una giovane coppia. Fino a settembre di quest'anno, ha vissuto con la mamma, la quale ha goduto di un lungo periodo di aspettativa.

Filomena, la mamma di Laura, é insegnante elementare e Giuseppe, il papà é dipendente dalla Amministrazione Provinciale in qualità di geometra.

Laura inizia la frequenza al nido, nella sezione Lattanti, a 10 mesi e mezzo.

Dal colloquio, svoltosi a fine agosto, prima di iniziare la frequenza al nido della bimba, tra noi e i genitori di Laura, abbiamo appreso che la piccola é nata a termine di una gravidanza normale con parto fisiologico, che é stata allattata al seno fino al terzo mese di vita, che non ha contratto mai alcuna malattia, ma che le é stata riscontrata una leggera lussazione all'anca, a causa della quale deve indossare una sostenuta "imbottitura" tra le gambe, che funge da divaricatore.

Questo fatto crea una leggera ansia nei genitori i quali hanno paura che la bimba, che sta cominciando ora a gatto-

nare, viva l'ambientamento al nido con più difficoltà anche a causa del fatto che é stato consigliato loro di non "sforzare" Laura.

THE DIARY AT THE INFANT-TODDLER CENTER
RECORDING THE STORY OF EACH CHILD

Story of Laura

It is an example of how the stories of the little ones can be recorded with the pen and the camera.

Who Is Laura?

Laura was born on October 13, 1980, the first child of a young couple. Until September of this year, 1981, she lived with her mother, who enjoyed a long leave from work. Her mother, Filomena, is an elementary teacher and her father, Giuseppe, is employed as a surveyor[1] by the Provincial Administration. Laura starts attending the school at ten and a half months in the infant room.

From the conversation held between us and the parents at the end of August, before the child started attending the center, we learned that the child was born at term of a normal pregnancy with natural delivery, was breastfed for three months, never contracted any disease, but that she was diagnosed with a slight hip dislocation, and because of that she has to wear a padded brace between her legs to keep them apart.

This fact makes the parents slightly anxious, as they are afraid that the child, who is now starting to crawl, will have more difficulties at the school, considering that the parents were advised not to "strain Laura."

---

1. Translator's note: there is no English equivalent for this degree-based position, somewhere between the position of an architect and a civil engineer.

2

Sempre al colloquio, Filomena e Giuseppe ci dicono che Laura ha un buon appetito e che non ha mai creato problemi per l'alimentazione; sebbene non abbia alcun dentino comincia a masticare ed accetta di assaggiare ogni alimento nuovo che le venga proposto.

Per andare a dormire usa un ciuccio rotondo ed esige che qualcuno rimanga accanto a lei accarezzandole la mano; secondo i genitori si risveglia di buon umore.

COSA E' IL DIARIO

Le annotazioni che seguono, sui primi due mesi al nido di Laura, sono parte di un "diario", redatto per ciascun bambino della sezione. Il reparto Lattanti é composto di 12 bambini (l'età varia dai 4 ai 12 mesi). Ogni bambino ha pertanto un "diario" personale esposto assieme agli altri in un unico pannello che ci accompagna fin dall'inizio dell'anno scolastico, che nasce da una duplice esigenza:

1) Fissare per noi, come strumento di osservazione perpetua, lo sviluppo del bambino nei suoi vari aspetti e nelle sue diverse modificazioni, che altrimenti, per la loro veloce evoluzione, rischierebbero di andare perdute.

2) Dare alla famiglia la documentazione di come il proprio bambino viva il nido, documentazione che alla fine dell'anno e della frequenza al nido nella sua globalità vorremmo con

segnare alla famiglia stessa, anche per offrire al bambino, più in là nel tempo, la possibilità di ricostruire la propria storia attraverso le parole e le immagini che gli abbiamo registrato durante la sua frequenza al nido.

La documentazione é a cura di Eluccia e Ivetta, le due assistenti della sezione.

During the conversation, the parents also told us that Laura has a good appetite and that she has never had any eating problems. Even though she doesn't have any teeth yet, she is starting to chew, and she is willing to try any new food that is given to her.

When she goes to bed, she takes a round pacifier and demands that somebody stay with her and stroke her hand. According to the parents she wakes up in a good mood.

What Is the Diary?

The following annotations on Laura's first two months at the infant-toddler center are part of a diary that was compiled for each child in the room. The infant room includes twelve children (aged from four to twelve months old). Each child has a personal diary displayed with the others in a display case;

this diary accompanies us from the beginning of the year and stems from a double need:

1. *To record for us, as an ongoing observational tool, the development of the child in its various aspects and changes, a development that otherwise would risk getting lost because of the child's quick evolution.*
2. *To give the family a documentation of how the child lives his or her experience, a documentation that at the end of the year and at completion of attendance is given to the family in its entirety, which also gives the child the opportunity to later reconstruct his or her story through the words and the images recorded during the time at the infant-toddler center.*

The documentation is collected by Eluccia and Ivetta, the two educators in the room.

3

4 SETTEMBRE: L'AIUTO DEI PENSILI

E' il primo giorno di "scuola". Laura arriva al nido con la mamma e la nonna paterna. La nonna, che in un primo momento rimane fuori, invitata dalla nuora entra nel nido per conoscerlo e visitarlo. L'accompagna nella visita proprio la nuora, che ha già avuto l'occasione di visitare con noi il nido, nel colloquio di fine agosto.

Seduta sul tappeto rosso, in sezione, Laura appare serena: ascolta attentamente i rumori dei "pensili", che lei stessa tocca e muove e i suoni degli strumenti musicali che io provoco.

Alessandro e Agnese, che le sono vicini sul tappeto, non paiono interessarla. La mamma e la nonna ritornano in sezione: vedono Laura tranquilla e "alla chetichella" si

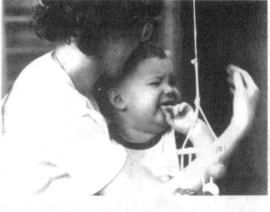

allontanano. Laura é ancora concentrata nei suoi giochi, ma quando si rende conto dell'assenza della mamma, scoppia a piangere ed io non so come arginare questo primo pianto.

Prendo Laura tra le braccia, la accarezzo e tento di risolvere la "crisi" con l'espediente della distrazione.

Ricorro ai pensili, coi quali avevamo 'giocato' fino a poco prima. Li muovo, li offro a Laura, glieli faccio toccare; gliene faccio sentire i rumori ancora nuovi, fino a che Laura, pian piano, riesce a rilassarsi, a sorridere alle palline colorate e a lanciarle davanti a sé, seguendo il dondolìo.
(Eluccia)

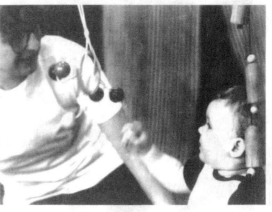

SEPTEMBER 4
HELP FROM THE MOBILES

t's the first day of "school." Laura arrives at the center with Mom and Grandma. The grandmother stays at first outside, but the daughter-in-law encourages her to come in to visit the center. She joins her daughter-in-law, who has already visited the center at the time of the meeting held at the end of August.

Sitting on the red carpet in the room, Laura appears to be happy. She listens attentively to the noise of the mobiles she touches and moves and to the sounds I make with the musical instruments.

Alessandro and Agnese, next to her on the carpet, do not seem to capture her interest. The mother and the grandmother go to the back of the room; they see Laura is

calm and they slip out [of the room]. Laura is still concentrating on her toys, but when she realizes that her mother is gone, she bursts into tears and I am not sure how to calm this first cry.

I pick her up, caress her, and try to solve the "crisis" using distraction.

I resort to the mobiles we just played with a moment ago. I move them, present them to Laura, I have her touch them; I let her hear the noises still new to her, until Laura, little by little, starts relaxing, smiling at the colorful balls, and throwing them in front of her, following their motion.

(Eluccia)

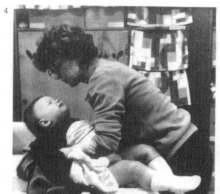

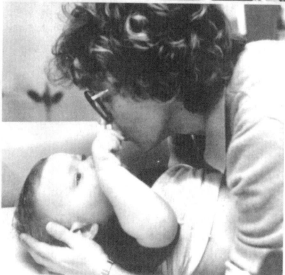

7 SETTEMBRE   LE DIFFICOLTA' DEL CAMBIO

Qualche difficoltà anche oggi per il momento del cambio. Devo infatti compiere più tentativi per farlo con relativa tranquillità della bimba. Quando tento di sdraiarla sul fasciatoio, Laura irrigidisce, come già da ieri, la schiena. La rialzo, la coccolo, tento di nuovo, ma ad un ulteriore irrigidimento, accompagnato da un accenno di pianto, la riprendo in braccio e torniamo in sezione. Provo un poco più tardi, anche perché Laura é molto bagnata.

Cerco di essere più cauta. La faccio sedere sul fasciatoio e parlo con lei, le mostro un giocattolo. Poi la rialzo in piedi e le tolgo i calzoncini. La lavo aiutandomi con un asciugamano bagnato e, solo in un secondo momento, cerco di accomodarla sul fasciatoio. La bimba si afferra con la mano al bordo del fasciatoio, un po' meno rigida di prima ma ugualmente "tirata".

La accompagno col mio corpo, tenendola abbracciata, vicina e la guardo, le parlo sottovoce. Lentamente, sdraiata, si rilassa e..... si accorge dei miei occhiali. (Eluccia)

SEPTEMBER 7
DIFFICULTIES DURING DIAPER CHANGE

Some difficulties today again at the moment of diaper change. I have to try a number of times to make sure I do not upset the child too much. When I try to lay her down on the changing table, Laura becomes stiff, as she did yesterday. I pick her back up, I cuddle her, I try again but when she becomes stiff again and almost starts to cry, I pick her back up and we return to the room. A little later I try again, considering that Laura is very wet.

I try to be more careful. I let her sit on the changing table and I talk to her. I show her a toy. I make her stand back up and I pull her pants down. I wash her using a wet cloth and only after a while do I try to lay her down on the changing table. The child grabs the side of the table, a little less rigid than before but still tense.

I follow her with my body, keep holding her close, I look at her, I talk to her quietly. Slowly while lying down, she relaxes and starts noticing my glasses.
(Eluccia)

5

17 SETTEMBRE   IL PRIMO BACIO AL PAPA'

Oggi, per la prima volta, Laura arriva al nido accompagnata dal papà. Con lui, che tiene Laura in braccio, scambio notizie ed impressioni sull'andamento dell'inserimento di Laura, che sembra procedere bene.

Mentre mi chiede consigli su come dovrà svolgersi il "distacco" dalla bimba, comincia a spogliarla togliendole il golfino e il berretto.

Giuseppe mi chiede come Laura affronti il pranzo ed il sonno e quali rapporti abbia intrecciato la bimba coi coetanei, poi me la affida.

Saluta la figlia che, invitata a farlo, ricambia il saluto e dà anche un bacio, sorprendendomi positivamente perché é solo da pochi giorni che Laura vive il distacco da chi l'accompagna (e fino ad ora é stata la mamma a farlo) più serenamente.

(Ivetta)

SEPTEMBER 17

THE FIRST KISS TO DADDY

Today for the first time Laura arrives at the infant-toddler center with Dad. He's holding her while I share information and impressions on how Laura is doing. She seems to be doing well.

While he is asking me for advice on what to do when he has to leave, he takes off her jacket and hat.

Giuseppe asks me how Laura does at lunchtime and naptime. He also asks about her relationships with peers, and then he hands her to me.

He tells her "bye" and invites her to say "bye" to him. She does so and gives him a kiss, which surprises me positively because it has only been a few days since Laura has started experiencing the departure of her mom positively (until now it was always Mom to drop her off).

(Ivetta)

6   29 SETTEMBRE   LA BAMBOLINA CONTROVERSA

Laura é Silvia (1), vicine sul tappeto della sezione "Piccoli" (2), giocano con oggetti diversi. Laura ha in mano una bambolina morbida, che contiene un sonaglio.

Quando Silvia la vede, la vuole, cerca di strapparla a Laura che, dopo una breve resistenza, cede la bambola scoppiando in un pianto disperato.

Silvia assiste, ma non si scompone, anzi guarda Laura piangere, ma continua a stringere la bambolina.

Solo il mio intervento riporta un po' di calma nelle due bimbe che, sempre vicine, indicano secondo le mie richieste, gli occhi, il naso, i capelli della bambola.

E' la prima volta che Laura litiga per il possesso di un giocattolo. (Eluccia).

_____

(1) Silvia é nata lo stesso giorno di Laura. Ha perciò 11 mesi e mezzo, appunto come Laura.

(2) La sezione "Piccoli" cui i bimbi Lattanti possono accedere in qualsiasi momento della giornata, é attigua alla sezione Lattanti e comunica con essa, attraverso il bagno, che é comune alle due sezioni, e attraverso la grande pedana di legno ricoperta di moquette, esterna alle due sezioni. Compongono la sezione "Piccoli" 14 bambini, la cui età varia, alla fine di settembre, dai 12 ai 18 mesi.

SEPTEMBER 29

THE CONTESTED DOLL

Laura and Silvia[1] are next to each other on the carpet of the Piccoli[2] (Little Ones) room and play with different objects. Laura holds a little soft doll that has a rattle inside.

When Silvia sees it, she wants it and tries to take it from Laura. Laura resists briefly, then gives up the doll and bursts into desperate tears.

Silvia witnesses this without reacting: she watches Laura cry but goes on holding onto the doll.

Only my intervention restores a little calmness between the little girls who, still next to each other, respond to my requests to point at the eyes, the nose, the hair of the doll.

This is the first time that Laura argues over a toy.
(Eluccia)

---

1. Silvia was born on the same day as Laura. Therefore she is exactly eleven and a half months like Laura [note in the original text].

2. The *Piccoli* room is next to the room of the *Lattanti* and connected to it through the changing room, which is shared by the two rooms, and also through a long, wooden, carpeted passageway, which is outside of the two rooms. Infants from the *Lattanti* can go to the *Piccoli* room at any time during the day. In the *Piccoli* room there are fourteen children whose ages vary at the end of September from ten to eighteen months old [note in the original text]. [Editors' note: Laura is in the infant room, or *Lattanti*. Children are part of the same group from September to June, but at Arcobaleno (and at other infant-toddler centers), the *Lattanti* and *Piccoli* rooms are located very close to one another, and the children in these two groups often spend time together and their teachers collaborate. The ages of the children in each group can vary a little from year to year, but usually the *Lattanti* are aged about three to ten months in September. *Piccoli* children are aged about ten months to eighteen months, *Medi* children are aged about eighteen to twenty-four months, and *Grandi* children are aged about twenty-four to thirty-six months.]

7

30 SETTEMBRE   IL PRIMO GIOCO IMITATIVO

Racconto a Filomena, che que
sta mattina accompagna Laura,del
litigio di ieri per il   possesso
della bambolina.

Mi dice che a casa, da qualche giorno, lei e la bimba gioca
no con una bambola di stoffa a
farle la ninna-nanna.

E la nostra sorpresa é grande quando, do
po il sonno mattutino, Laura, serena e rilas
sata, prende tra le braccia una bambola e,se
duta nell'angolo del cucù, se la stringe in
braccio cullandola, sorridendole, toccandole
il naso e, dondolandosi avantie indietro,pro
nuncia "nana nana".

Ma la sorpresa non finisce perché Laura
scorge ai suoi piedi uno dei cucchiaini che
sono in sezione nel cesto del "tesori" di me
tallo.

Lo afferra e comincia ad "imboccare" la
bambola poi, dopo un attimo di esitazione,
guarda il cucchiaio e lo porta alla propria
bocca.

L'atteggiamento così sereno di Laura ci
dà la misura di quanto abbia accettato noi e •
il nido e che il suo ambientamento sta proce
dendo bene; ci consente inoltre di prendere
atto che Laura sta avviando il gioco imitati
vo. Una grande conquista! (Eluccia e Ivetta)

SEPTEMBER 30
THE FIRST IMITATION GAME

This morning when Filomena drops off Laura, I tell her about yesterday's argument over the little doll.

She tells me that at home they have been playing for a few days with a stuffed doll, cuddling it to sleep.

So we were very surprised and pleased when, after the morning nap, Laura, who is calm and relaxed, takes a doll in her arms and sits in the cuckoo corner, holding it tight, rocking, smiling, touching the doll's nose, and singing nighty-night.

But we were even more surprised and interested when Laura discovers at her feet one of the spoons that are in the room in the basket of metal treasures.

She grabs it and starts feeding the doll, then, after a little hesitation, looks at the spoon and takes it to her mouth.

Laura's happy attitude shows how she has accepted us and the infant-toddler center and that she is adjusting well. We're also noticing that Laura is starting imitation games. What a great conquest!
(Eluccia and Ivetta)

8

2 OTTOBRE   LA MELA IN CUCINA

Filomena, al suo arrivo con Laura ci annuncia che ieri sera, a casa, Laura ha mosso da sola due passi. Duran

te la mattina, insieme ai bimbi del reparto "Piccoli" andiamo in salone (1). Laura si aggrappa alle mie gambe e mi tira verso il refettorio dei Medi e dei Grandi, che comunica con la cucina del nido con una grande porta a vetrata. Accompagno Laura verso il vetro. Mi segue Giorgio, che già cammina da solo. Accomodo tutti e due sul parapetto della vetrata per permettere loro di osservare meglio, da un'altezza maggiore, ciò che Wilma, la cuoca, e Marisa, l'aiutocuoca, stanno facendo in cucina. Poi entriamo.

Laura e Giorgio appaiono incuriositi dall'ambiente: ne seguono i rumori. Faccio sedere i due bambini sul bancone dove Ma

risa sta preparando la frutta per il pranzo. Marisa mette loro davanti un canovaccio poi offre a ciascuno un pezzettino di mela che, dopo un breve attimo di esitazione, accettano e iniziano a mordere e a succhiare.

Sono talmente assorti ed intenti a gustare la frutta che posso allontanarmi dalla cucina senza suscitare alcuna reazione né in Laura né in Giorgio, che torno poi a prendere dopo qualche minuto e che ritrovo sul bancone ancora intenti a seguire Marisa e Wilma e con in mano un nuovo pezzo di mela.

(Eluccia)

(1) Il salone é un'ampia area del nido in cui trovano spazio i grandi attrezzi: un dondolo, due "gabbie" che pendono dal soffitto, una "casetta" che consente a chi vi entra di isolarsi dagli altri, uno scivolo, una grande pedana a gradoni di altezze diverse.

Sul salone si affacciano le altre due sezioni che compongono il nido: la sezione dei Medi e la sezione dei Grandi, formate rispettivamente di 19 e 23 bambini, seguiti da 3 + 3 assistenti.

OCTOBER 2

THE APPLE IN THE KITCHEN

Filomena arrives with Laura and announces that last night at home Laura had taken her first two steps.

During the morning we take the children from the Piccoli room to the piazza.[1] Laura grabs my legs and pulls me to the dining area of the Medi and Grandi, which is connected to the kitchen of the infant-toddler center through a big glass door. I take Laura to the glass. Giorgio, who can already walk, follows us. I have them both stand in front of the glass so that they can watch at a better height what Wilma, the cook, and Marisa, the assistant cook, are doing in the kitchen. Then we go in.

Laura and Giorgio seem very curious about this environment and follow its noises. I have the children sit on the counter where Marisa is preparing the fruit for lunch. Marisa puts towels around their necks, and then gives them little slices of apple, and after a little hesitation they accept them and start chewing and sucking on them.

They are so absorbed and intent on tasting the fruit that I leave the kitchen without either of them reacting. Then after a few minutes I come back and I find them on the counter still watching Marisa and Wilma and with the new apple slices.

(Eluccia)

---

1. The *piazza* is a wide area in the infant-toddler center where the big pieces of equipment are located: a seesaw, two open structures that children can enter made of wood and ropes crossed together that hang from the ceiling and are secured to the floor, a toy house that allows a child to take a break from the others, a slide, and a big board with steps of different heights. The two rooms of the center are adjacent to the *piazza*: the *Medi* room (for middle children) and the *Grandi* room (for the big children) composed respectively of nineteen and twenty-three children, with three-plus-three teachers [note in the original text].

9

9 OTTOBRE   L A U R A   E   L O   S P E C C H I O

Laura é sul tappeto, in sezione, di fronte allo specchio. Gioca coi piccoli oggetti di legno presi da uno dei cesti dei "tesori".

La sua immagine riflessa la cattura e Laura comincia tutta una serie di movimenti a destra e a sinistra seguendo l'immagine dello specchio. Allunga la mano destra, poi la sinistra finché, evidentemente soddisfatta, si sorride e si "parla" con vocalizzi ed esclamazioni: "Biii! Beee!"

Più tardi Filomena ci conferma che usa queste esclamazioni anche con lei a casa, per tutte le cose e gli avvenimenti che la sorprendono.

(Ivetta)

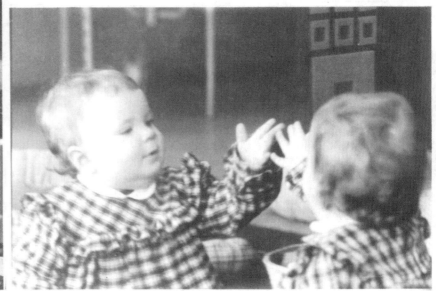

OCTOBER 9

LAURA AND THE MIRROR

Laura is in the room on the carpet in front of the mirror. She is playing with the small wooden objects she took from one of the treasure baskets.

Her reflection catches her attention and Laura starts moving left and right, following her image in the mirror. She stretches out her right hand, then her left. She must be content because she smiles and talks to herself with babbling and exclamations, "Beeeeeee!!! Baaaaaaaaa!!!"

Later, Filomena confirms that she uses these exclamations at home, too, for all those events that surprise her.

(Ivetta)

10 <u>12 OTTOBRE</u> <u>A L L A   S C O P E R T A   D E L   C A S S E T T O</u>

Il cassetto della scrivania, semiaperto, atti
ra Laura, che vi si avvicina incuriosita. Laura
cammina da qualche giorno e, in piedi, arriva al
la scrivania: dopo aver aperto un po' di più il
cassetto e dopo averlo "perlustrato", inclinando
il viso, afferra un foglio di carta. Ma é un foglio lunghissimo di etichette adesive e Laura ti
ra, tira, tira con ampi movimenti del braccio, fin
ché il foglio finisce. I piedi di Laura sono som
mersi dalla carta e il cassetto ora é vuoto. Lau
ra verifica che di carta proprio non ce ne sia più
Riguarda tutta la striscia ai suoi piedi, la sol
leva, ma questo nuovo gioco non pare entusiasmar
la. Quello che pare la interessi é riprendere e re
plicare il gioco del tirar fuori, per questo,con
una relazione per noi piuttosto ardita,apre l'al
tro cassetto, guardandomi poi interrogativa perché lo trova vuoto.Non convinta riapre quello di
sopra (il primo), lo ricontrolla con lo sguardo poi,
con aria delusa si allontana. (Eluccia, Ivetta)

OCTOBER 12

DISCOVERING THE DRAWER

The desk drawer is half open and Laura becomes curious and goes closer. Laura has been walking for a few days, and standing, reaches the desk. After opening the drawer a little more, and exploring it, she tilts her head and grabs a piece of paper. It's a very long paper with sticky labels, and Laura keeps pulling and pulling with large movements of the arm until the paper is all out. Laura's feet are completely covered by the paper and the drawer is empty. Laura makes sure that there is no more paper in the drawer. She then looks at the long strip at her feet and picks it up, but she does not seem to think that this game is very exciting. What she finds interesting to repeat is the "emptying" game, and so she makes a connection (quite a brave one, we think), and she opens the other drawer, but then she looks puzzled because she finds it empty. She is not convinced and she reopens the first drawer above, checks it again, and then she leaves, disappointed.
(Eluccia, Ivetta)

Usciamo in cortile. Assieme ad altri bim
bi Laura viene fatta salire sul "passeggio
ne" (1) del nido e percorriamo così i viot
toli intorno al nido. Laura,dapprima cauta
(si tiene stretta ai bordi del carretto ed
ai cuscini che ne imbottiscono le pareti),
in breve si mostra entusiasta del viaggio.
Scorge, attraverso le vetrate i bimbi gran
di e Cinzia e li saluta con grandi gesti del
braccio e ampi sorrisi.Loro ricambiano con
altrettanto entusiasmo. Arrivati nei pressi
della cucina il "rituale" si ripete. Laura
e gli altri bimbi salutano Wilma attraverso la finestra e Wilma non solo ci saluta,
ma esce venendoci incontro e aiuta i bimbi
a scendere dal "passeggione".   (Eluccia)

bi piccoli, che non sanno cammina
re, o che si stancherebbero pre-

sto, contemporaneamente.

(1) Il passeggione é un carretto costruito
per il nido da un gruppo di genitori.Ci con
sente di fare passeggiate anche con più bim

OCTOBER 13

ON BOARD THE BIG STROLLER

We go out in the yard together with other children. Laura is placed up on the big "stroller"[1] of the school and we walk in the alleys around the center. Laura is cautious at first, holding tight to the side of the cart and to the pillows that pad it, but soon she becomes excited about the trip. She sees through the glass the big children and Cinzia, a teacher of the Grandi class, and she greets them with big movements of the arms and big smiles. They greet her back with the same enthusiasm. When they arrive close to the kitchen, the "ritual" is repeated. Laura and the other children greet Wilma through the window and Wilma not only greets them back but this time she comes out towards us and helps the children getting off the "stroller."
(Eluccia)

---

1. The stroller is a cart built for the center by a group of parents. It allows us to go on a walk with many small children who cannot walk or would be too tired too soon at the same time [note in the original text].

12

21 OTTOBRE   IL TIC-TAC DELL'OROLOGIO

A tavola,finito di mangiare, la situazione é molto serena. I bimbi "giocano" tra loro, "parlottano". Approfittando di questa tranquillità offro a Laura un grosso catalogo ricco di immagini e la invito a sfogliarlo. Nel farlo la bimba é molto attenta, non alza mai lo sguardo dalle illustrazioni,che scorre con interesse e, quando deve voltare la pagina, lo fa con cura e finezza di movimenti.

Non intervengo per non disturbarla, tanto é assorta. La guardo. Indica le immagini di uomini e donne coi vocaboli "mamma" e "papà" che pronuncia a voce bassa.

Davanti a una serie di orologi, mi guarda: mi avvicino e li guardo con lei: "sono orologi", le dico e le mostro quello che ho al polso. Glielo avvicino al

l'orecchio e può udirne il ticchettio: lo ascolta a lungo, attenta,poi stacca l'orecchio, si rialza, rivolge lo sguardo alle immagini, le fissa di nuovo e poi, decisa, vi accosta l'orecchio.

(Eluccia).

OCTOBER 21

THE WATCH'S TICK-TOCK

*A*t the table after eating, everybody is very happy. The children play with each other and "talk." Taking advantage of this tranquility, I offer to Laura a big catalog full of images and I encourage her to flip through it. While she is doing that she is very intent, she never takes her eyes off the images, and she goes through these images with interest. When she turns the page, her movements are very careful and refined.

I do not interfere so as not to disturb her because she is so intent. I watch her. She points to the images of men and women, saying quietly the words "mommy" and "daddy."

In front of a line of watches, she looks at me; I go closer and I look at them with her. I tell her, "They are watches," and I show her the one on my wrist. I put it close to her ear so she can hear the tick-tock. She listens for a long time, intent, then she moves her ear away, pulls her head up, goes back to the images, stares at them again, and then with confidence, puts her ear next to the page. (Eluccia)

Introduzione di CARLA RINALDI, dell'Equipe Pedagogico-Didattica
        dei Nidi e Scuole dell'Infanzia Comunali di Reggio E.
Testi e foto a cura di GIULIANA CAMPANI, IVETTA FORNACIARI,
        ELUCCIA FORGHIERI dell'Asilo Nido Comunale "ARCOBALENO"
        di Reggio Emilia
Grafica di CARLA NIRONI
Stampato a cura del CENTRO STAMPA COMUNALE di Reggio Emilia

Introduction written by Carlina Rinaldi of the Pedagogical Team for the Infant-Toddler Centers and Preschools of Reggio Emilia

Contents by Giuliana Campani, Ivetta Fornaciari, and Eluccia Forghieri, of the Arcobaleno Infant-Toddler Center

Graphics by Carla Nironi

Published by the Print Center, Municipality of Reggio Emilia, March 1983

(Translated into English by Silvia Betta, University of Nebraska–Lincoln, 2006)

Part Three

A REUNION AT ARCOBALENO

An Encounter with Laura

Giuliana Campani, Paola Cavazzoni, Eluccia Forghieri, and Tiziana Bini
Arcobaleno Infant-Toddler Center
Reggio Emilia, Italy
(Translated by Silvia Betta)

Eluccia, Giuliana, Paola, and Tiziana Meet Laura, Davide, and Filomena

Laura is twenty-six years old, is married, and has a child, Davide, who is almost three years old. After many years she has come back to the Arcobaleno Infant-Toddler Center, bringing her son, Davide, and her mother, Filomena. Both Laura and her mother accept with joy and curiosity our invitation to trace back with us, through the diary, Laura's experience at the center.

We greet her right at the entrance of the center, where the image sequence, "Laura and the Watch," has been displayed for a few years, an exhibition that has her as keen protagonist, together with Eluccia, one of her teachers. Laura tells us how she graduated from secondary school (a school with preparation programs for the fields of psychology and teaching[1]) and how she studied the violin.

---

1. The Liceo Psicopedagogico is a secondary school that students attend for five years, one year more than the typical U.S. high school. It focuses on specific disciplines and prepares students for university study in those fields.

We take her, Davide, and Filomena around the rooms of the center, and she comments on the size of the spaces, and how she perceives them as smaller than when she was attending: "I remember everything bigger . . . the environment and the objects, even the drawers." She seems to recall many of the structures and the equipment in the *piazza* (central square). "I remember very well this piece of equipment, but it was decorated with different colors, and a big central stripe . . . I remember when my friend, Francesca, and I were lying in the pyramid of mirrors, thinking about our transition to preschool, and how we were sad about leaving the infant-toddler center."

We finally sit down in the *atelier* (studio), a space that is central to the infant-toddler center design, and continue our dialogue on the past, the future, and us, with

Baby Laura, now a young married mother living in Tuscany, is welcomed back to Arcobaleno Infant-Toddler Center. She stands (from left to right) with her infant son, Davide, her former teacher, Eluccia Forghieri, who wrote many diary entries, her mother, Filomena, and Giuliana Campani (far right), who was the teacher of the younger toddlers and collaborated with the two teachers of the infant group in taking photos and documenting.

the aid of images and documents. Coming into the studio brings Laura more memories connected to this space, "I really liked painting here, at the easel . . ."

We had first invited Laura back in 2001, when we celebrated the twenty-five-year anniversary of the Infant-Toddler Center Arcobaleno, because the image sequence "Laura and the Watch" has come to represent both in Italy and around the world our educational philosophy. It is the emblem of those concepts we have been mastering, studying, and perfecting for years, day after day. Laura is a bit our symbol, a symbol of which we are proud.

This new visit, too, takes us back in time and in our thoughts. What has changed since twenty-five years ago when Laura attended the center? What has changed again since six years ago when she came back to visit for the first time? What has changed about us, our philosophy, and our practice? What is it in the image sequence "Laura and the Watch" that has preserved its strength, its vigor, and its capacity for being read and reread with always renewed relevance?

The diary, whose original copy her mom, Filomena, has kept through the years, has been a precious memory of the life journey of Laura and her family. Looking through the pages of the diary with us again, a surprised Laura amazingly reveals how those events and situations captured by the photos are still present in her mind as living images, especially the stories about the paper pulled from the drawer and about the watch. These images make her shiver, and her mother, smiling next to her, provides her affectionate solidarity.

While looking through these diary pages for a long time, Laura reconstructs her memories of the time past, wondering how it was, remembering her dad, who appears shy in a photo of dropping her off in the morning, and remembering her sister, who had a similar and yet different experience at the center because she was here a few years later. She glances from her son, Davide, to her mom, Filomena. She tells us proudly about Davide's accomplishments, his constant activity, and her own hopes and expectations as a parent: "I see myself in him, even though I was perhaps not as active . . . my hope is that he will be intelligent and grow well."

Filomena in turn compares past and present. She tells us about her experience as a mother after moving to Reggio Emilia from a town far away in southern Italy. She has been able to renew herself as a woman, as a wife, as an elementary teacher, as a mother, and now as a grandmother. She recounts anecdotes of her response to what the center offered: "When I saw Arcobaleno, I remember I was happy because I liked this place for my daughter and I liked the atmosphere that was breathed here . . . You all have given me a real joy."

Recently, Laura was invited for a reunion at Arcobaleno Infant-Toddler Center.

Filomena is surprised when Giuliana reminds her of a statement she made during a parent-teacher meeting before the school opening that first September, a statement that made Giuliana reflect a lot and that had generated a new attitude in her and the group of educators at the center. It was after Giuliana had presented the issue of transitioning to the center and spoke about the possible feelings of difficulty and crisis that children and families might experience that Filomena optimistically pointed out how such difficulties would not necessarily arise, and suggested it was better not to stir anxiety in those who perhaps did not feel anxious.

She came with her mother, Filomena, and her infant son, Davide.

After many years, this statement confirms the importance of dialogue, the idea of mutual listening, and the need for children, educators, and parents to feel part of the infant-toddler center. Filomena's words also reinforce the idea that the images of Laura showing her feeding the doll or placing her ear on the paper clock in the magazine continue to suggest how observation of the child's gestures with materials, the environment, and peers enriches us as educators, as well as parents. This gives value to educa-

All three enjoyed poring over the pictures in Laura's infant diary.

At the reunion was Eluccia Forghieri (far left), one of Laura's old teachers, who wrote many of the diary entries. Tiziana Bini (second from left) is currently the cook at Arcobaleno Infant-Toddler Center, and Paola Cavazzoni (far right) coordinated the visit in her role as pedagogical coordinator for this center since 1993. Filomena, Davide, and Laura sit at the head of the table. Baby Davide likes feeding cake to his grandmother.

tional choices, opening to doubt, dialogue, change, and research. Laura and Filomena again confirmed this with the characteristic reserve they had before, but also with the same open smiles they showed when we said good-bye many years ago, at the end of their experience at the center.

Filomena describes how this experience increased her confidence even in her role as an elementary teacher, reinforcing how fundamental it is to listen to the child, the children together, and to encourage them, their questions, their curiosity, accepting the mutual uncertainties and trying together, constructing dialogues at the same level, supported by an environment that puts everybody "on the same level," as Filomena said when she visited the center with her aunt and mother-in-law at the time Laura was attending. For Filomena, the experience as a parent at the infant-toddler center represented an important transition, "an invitation to look at children from a different point of view and to recognize them as people."

Laura says good-bye with a smile and promises to come back. She regrets that Davide cannot enjoy an experience like the one she and her sister, Luisa, enjoyed at the infant-toddler center and then at the Preschool Anna Frank. We thank her, the person who became the emblem of a new child, because thanks to her we started looking at that child from a new perspective and with renewed senses. And we think back to the diary full of annotations, hoping each of the twelve infants of that year still preserves it as testimony of a research that involved them, their families, us, the idea of the child, and the idea of a new kind of early childhood center.

Laura and the Diary

After pausing to talk with Laura about the diary, that diary we began to compile in 1981 (published in 1983) and often revisited in the course of time as a tool and as a resource, we reflected among ourselves. We evaluated the passing of time and the evolution that has taken place as we reviewed what we do, our actions, our choices, our writings, our thoughts, in the light of what the pages of this tool contained and delivered in short-term and long-term time frames.

Laura's diary, then, just like that of Silvia, Andrea, or Elisa . . . of the infant room of Arcobaleno Infant-Toddler Center, strived to *find* the *real* child to whom nobody had paid attention until then, especially in an organization like the infant-toddler center, which was typically considered a service of assistance and care. Together with Carlina Rinaldi, the pedagogical coordinator of the center at that time, we contributed to the discovery of that small child we knew so little about beyond, that is, the growth charts, teething schedules, and developmental milestones. We made discoveries day after day through the observation of each child in relationship with the adults, other children, and materials, and also with the child herself, in her persistence in exploring and relating to the world.

We evaluated the passing of time.

Laura contributed to a more and more defined image of the child who knows and is able to do, who knows and is able to discover, suggest, involve, whenever the adult is also able to listen, see, suggest, relaunch, provoke, wonder, make hypotheses, and relate, and whenever an adult is able to document and fix in time the child's own curiosity, hypotheses, and questions, creating projects and contextualizing hypotheses and possible answers.

After so many years, this is what Laura and her diary continue to suggest. In those pages is the thread of our story, our research, our growth, our pauses, of the evolution of an educational program in a world that is quickly changing and allows different sources of knowledge and cultures to meet, hybridize, and join, a world in which categories of space and time change as technology rapidly evolves, where even the values of communication and society are changing, thus contributing to the construction of always new identities of the person, the city and its services, and the concept of early childhood and early childhood educational services.

Today, we still compile a diary for each of the children at the infant-toddler center. It is a diary that has undergone a great evolution of content and project. Its current focus is both a child with whom it is possible to dare, because he wants to dare, as well as a child we can read in his relationship with the materials, the environment, with us, with peers, a child who daily constructs his knowledge through the many languages that we learned to value, even though we still have a long way to go in this sense.

Laura gave us testimony of how each child possesses relational associations, knowledge, and research strategies of his or her own, strategies that are supported and valued by the environment, environment as network of relationships as well as structural environment. This awareness makes us adults responsible for rereading every day our gestures, hypotheses, and theories, in order to reinforce the dialogue, exchange, and construction of knowledge of the earliest childhood, an age for which a lot remains yet to be understood.

In conclusion, Laura's diary revealed itself as and still remains a huge opportunity to reflect not only on our role as teachers, but also on our identity as women in an ever-changing society and school.

Giuliana Campani and *Eluccia Forghieri* have been teachers since 1976 at the Arcobaleno Infant-Toddler Center in Reggio Emilia. *Paola Cavazzoni* is the current pedagogical coordinator at Arcobaleno. *Tiziana Bini* is the cook at Arcobaleno.

Part Four

REFLECTIONS
FROM AROUND THE WORLD

How the Infant Teacher's Context Influences the Content of Diaries

J. Ronald Lally
Center for Child and Family Studies, WestEd
San Francisco, California, USA

*I*n 2003, I attended a meeting in Reggio Emilia with teachers and *pedagogistas* (the educational coordinators, each responsible for a certain number of preschools and infant-toddler centers in the municipal system). A member of a visiting group of Americans happened to use the terms *caregiver* and *provider* in asking a question about infant care practice. There was a pause and then a *pedagogista* offered these ideas in a memorable exchange:

"Why do you use those words?"

"Why don't you use the term *teacher*?"

"Here we don't want somebody just taking care of people or providing a service—somebody following a manual."

"We want creative thinkers to be with our children, not technicians, people who will form hypotheses about the effect of their actions and entertain the hypotheses of the children."

"With our children, we want adults who can think on their feet."

That exchange was one of many that week that helped show the subtle, and sometimes not so subtle, differences between infant-toddler child care practice in the United States[1] and in Reggio Emilia.

In this essay, I will use *Story of Laura* as the basis for highlighting some current differences in practice. By looking at Laura's diary, we can parse out many of these differences, because the diary contains not only perceptive insights into Laura's experience and keys to how to facilitate those experiences, but also a way to examine the context in which the diary is written. It is my premise that duplicating a diary process in U.S. classrooms without clearly understanding the context and motivation from which the diary is developed would result in outcomes varying from those produced in Reggio Emilia (Lally 2001). The purpose for this exposition is to warn against an empty duplication of technique and to make sure that Americans understand what they are, and what they are not, importing when they import practice. If diaries are to become a successful tool in the United States, adapters must examine their own context and how it influences the diary process, because philosophical and technical grounding, program policies, staff training, and educators' vision of the role of the child and the role of the teacher will frame and provoke what they create (Lally and Mangione 2006; Lally, Mangione, and Greenwald 2006).

What follows are three distinctions between general infant-toddler practice in the United States and Reggio Emilia that tend to alter both the content and use of diaries.

---

1. In this essay, general reference is made to infant-toddler child care in the United States. It is recognized by the author that many different types of care and of training for care are available throughout the United States. My statements refer to services normally available, not to model or demonstration programs.

Observation Training: The Distinction between Participant and Nonparticipant Observation Practices

One obvious, but not often discussed, training difference between the United States and Reggio Emilia is the distinction between styles of observation training. Although a number of U.S. colleges and universities have expanded observation training to include practices similar to those used in Reggio Emilia, in most college classrooms in the United States, particularly psychology and child development classes, students are trained to observe as nonparticipating objective observers. They are instructed to sit silently, be as unobtrusive and invisible as possible, record things that are factual, and exclude assumptions, predictions, and interpretation. In the introduction to Laura's diary (pages 22–27), you'll see that the teacher is instructed to do exactly the opposite. In Reggio Emilia, the teachers are asked to participate actively with the children, to take notes on the fly, to selectively record things that they think will have meaning both for their use and for the child's and the child's family's use at a later time. They are also asked to be subjective and interpretive in their note taking and to focus on dynamics that arise in relationships. These two different observational strategies place value on different types of information. In Reggio Emilia, the teachers are asked to use themselves as instruments and to record what they think has meaning. In the United States, teachers are asked to collect raw data that anyone can interpret. Naturally these two approaches lead to vastly different diaries.

Reading Laura's diary suggests to me that if infant care teachers move to the use of diaries in the United States, their observation training must first be revolutionized. The introductory pages to the diary clearly point out this subjective observation technique. I see those wise words as a blueprint for that revolution.

Lesson Planning: The Distinction between Planning Lessons for Children and Developing Plans to Assist Children to Engage Their Topics of Interest

In recent years in the United States, school-readiness concerns and educational interventions have reached younger and younger children. Yet much of the theory driving the practice of teaching comes from the vision of children as "blank slates." This viewpoint sees children as lacking curiosity and motivation for learning about important topics and devoid of a learning agenda of their own. From this perspective, it is assumed that young children need lessons developed for them. "Filling" the child is seen as very serious work, and tracking progress requires a great deal of record keeping. For example, teachers assess children to discover which areas of their development are lacking and then craft lessons for each child. Lesson plans are written, assessments are filled out, progress as related to standards is charted, and accountings of time on task are recorded. From this point of view, the planning and conduct of lessons is the teacher's primary responsibility, and maintaining order for focus on these lessons is a major focus.

The child's learning agenda needs to be uncovered.

In Reggio Emilia, in contrast, the dominant vision of the child is not one of a "blank slate" but rather one of a motivated, curious meaning seeker who spends time constructing knowledge. Lessons don't have to be planned. Rather the child's learning agenda needs to be uncovered, respected, and assisted. In Reggio Emilia, diaries and similar forms of documentation are the main type of data collected. The teachers do less of the type of record keeping necessary to a "blank slate" view of the child because they don't see that as necessary. Yet they use diaries and similar documentation for many purposes, including to better understand each child and to create a valuable history of the child for teacher, child, and family use and enjoyment. Diaries are not seen as onerous extra work.

In the United States, classroom teachers commonly report they are so consumed by record keeping that they feel as though they have no time left to be with children. Why is this so different from the feeling about diary keeping you get while reading about Laura and her teachers? Again, it is context: the mind-set of teachers and administrators is different when they are planning lessons to fill "blank slates" than when they are finding ways to help children engage in and expand on lessons of their own choice. Context thus influences the value that teachers place on diaries and other forms of recording and documenting. In Reggio Emilia, the diary is a major and well-used documentation tool. In the United States, given the current "blank slate" vision of children, other types of documenting and assessing are seen as necessary, and if a diary were to be collected, it would most likely add to rather than replace records already collected. Given many U.S. teachers' perceptions that record keeping is a barrier to interaction with children, the last thing they would want to do is to be required to fill more pieces of paper.

Once again contexts generate use of diaries and perceptions of the value of diaries. As you read *Story of Laura*, look below its words to the core visions of the teaching/learning process and you will find much to learn there.

Orientation toward the Infant: The Distinction between the Infant as a "Subject of Love" Engaged in Exploration and the Infant as Receiver of Tender Loving Care or Intellectual Stimulation

In the United States, infant-toddler child care programs often look like either watered-down versions of preschool or a glorified version of babysitting. Indeed, what is too often seen is the implementation of curriculum extremes. One extreme is based on the belief that very young children only need safe environments and tender loving care and that specific attention to learning is inappropriate. The other extreme is based on the belief that for infants to grow and develop cognitively, they must be stimulated intellectually by adult-developed and adult-directed lessons and activities that are carefully planned ahead of time and programmed into the infants' day. In the middle lie only a few, cutting-edge programs that proclaim tender, loving, relationship-based care as part and parcel of intellectual development and language development.

In the first few introductory pages of Laura's diary, I was struck by the developmentally balanced stance taken by the philosophers, educators, and citizens of Reggio Emilia. That brief introduction written by Carlina Rinaldi in 1983 epitomizes what is at the core of the Reggio Emilia approach and what makes that approach so special. It makes visible the "heart" that underlies brilliant educational practice when it states that for a child in care, the use of a personalized diary helps to give the child the awareness of being a "subject of love." To me, this emotional gift to treat each child as a subject of love is key to everything that undergirds all the brilliant scientific exploration of teachers and children that we have come to know in Reggio Emilia. Teachers in

Treat each child as a subject of love.

Reggio Emilia take as a given that they should be subjectively relating to the children they serve—in the child's corner, so to speak, rooting for the child to succeed, giving him or her the benefit of the doubt, celebrating masteries, treating child-generated hypotheses as special, and creating loving and intellectually rich climates in which each child can joyfully experience each day in care. They are not babysitting or detachedly preparing the child for productive adult functioning. They simultaneously love them and cognitively engage them.

It is almost invisible to those who live it.

As Rinaldi states in *New Perspectives on Infant-Toddler Learning, Development, and Care*, "Learning and loving are not so far apart as we once thought" (Lally and WestEd 2006).

It is this deep wellspring of caring for children that is at the source of the curriculum excellence I see in Reggio Emilia classrooms. Yet in my travels to Reggio Emilia and in my conversations with teachers and *pedagogistas*, I seldom hear this caring discussed as a planned part of the approach. I believe that it is so completely taken for granted, so deeply engrained, that it is almost invisible to those who live it. It is so much a part of day-to-day life that it is barely discussed, so central to functioning that it is not seen.

Yet it is because teachers subjectively rather than objectively engage children that such pedagogical tools as diaries exist and prosper. Teachers want to give the child and the child's family a gift, a memory, a way to capture a period of the child's life that is precious and worth saving. Because of their affection for the children, teachers feel that they must capture what is going on in the day-to-day life of the child, so that they can better understand how to help this loved one prosper. These diaries are not seen as something extra to do but are done joyfully. Here once more we uncover the importance of context.

As we in other countries look at the use of diaries in our work with young children, we must first look deeply at the context in which we will develop diaries. Do we have the notion of the child as "subject of love" as a starting point of our diary work? Do we see our teaching role as assisting the children in engaging in their interests? Do we understand and value the role of participant-observer? The answers to these and other related questions will have a great deal to do with how much we can mine from *Story of Laura*.

Diaries must be seen as part of a bigger reality. It is the professional and personal use of diaries, rather than the recording of events, that makes them precious commodities.

J. Ronald Lally, EdD, has been developing programs and policies for young children and their families since 1966. He was a professor at Syracuse University and chair of its Department of Child and Family Studies for many years while directing its Family Development Research Program. For the past twenty-two years, he has directed the Program for Infant/Toddler Care (PITC) at WestEd in Sausalito, California. He is one of the founders and on the board of Zero to Three: National Center for Infants, Toddlers and Families. Most of his research deals with two topics: social-emotional development in infancy and the impact of early intervention on adult functioning. He has authored numerous publications, including his commentaries on Italian programs based on his visits to Reggio Emilia, Milan, and Pistoia.

Lally, J. Ronald, and WestEd. 2006. *New perspectives on infant/toddler learning, development, and care*. DVD, Disc 1. Sacramento: California Department of Education.

Lally, J. Ronald. 2001. Infant care in the United States and how the Italian experience can help. In *Bambini: The Italian approach to infant/toddler care*. Lella Gandini and Carolyn Edwards, eds. New York: Teachers College Press.

Lally, J. Ronald, and Peter L. Mangione. 2006. The uniqueness of infancy demands a responsive approach to care. *Young Children* 61 (4): 14–20.

Lally, J. Ronald, Peter L. Mangione, and Deborah Greenwald, eds. 2006. *Concepts for care: 20 essays on infant/toddler development and learning*. Sacramento: WestEd.

IN THE FOOTSTEPS OF LAURA'S TEACHERS

A SCOTTISH PERSPECTIVE

Pat Wharton
Early Learning Associates
Stirling, Scotland

Revisiting a diary published twenty years ago about Laura when she was a baby has several positive dimensions. Clearly for Laura and her family, it provides vivid traces and memories about that period in Laura's life, memories that are really important for her as an adult and now as a mother to make sense of in the context of her early life in the infant-toddler center. For educators, there are additional benefits. The idea of keeping a record of certain elements of a child's life in the early-years setting is becoming more usual in Scotland, but the particular way in which this diary is presented as an observational tool as well as a record of the child's early days in the early-years setting is in the main unusual. The unusual aspect is that observations tend to be the preserve of the educator, who uses them to support plans made for the child's learning. To endow infant observations with a dual purpose and present them as a reflection of Laura's early life outside the family context makes visible through these written and photographic recordings that part of her life that might otherwise have been lost to Laura herself and to her own children.

What makes this diary so compelling is its loving image of one particular child, coupled with the educators' deep understanding of the importance of tuning into and recording the child's progress toward maturity. For Laura herself, it can provide a historical platform from which she and her family can make connections and comparisons with future generations of children, while for those of us in Scotland working toward a deeper understanding of the process of documentation, it can serve as a guide to constructing a piece of documentation that can become a powerful memory of where the child has been. Currently in Scotland there is much debate about how to make meaningful connections with the child within the context of his or her home and the early-years setting. Laura's diary in its original form is one powerful example of this, and revisiting it twenty years later reminds us again that such a recording is not fixed in a particular place in time; instead, it is timeless.

Such a recording is not fixed in a particular place in time.

For one child's educational diary to call for translation and revisiting after twenty years suggests it holds something very special. In its pages we see how the pedagogical context within which it was conceived was underpinned by a loving image of the child, whose capabilities were documented with joy and whose needs were interpreted, understood, and supported by both the family and the educators. Today in Scotland, we are moving toward this way of thinking and being with our children and, therefore, the pedagogical context within which we are operating is in a process of transition (Kinney and Wharton 2007; Abbott and Nutbrown 2001). This diary has the ability to help us in our process of moving forward. The diary is a compelling piece of documentation even though it was constructed in a very straightforward and accessible way. Its very practical nature will be a helpful model for educators in furthering their understandings of observational methods, for example, in the way it is laid out in terms of the introduction to Laura and her family.

The Diary as Observational Record

To call this observational record a "diary" is of particular interest in itself. In Scotland, we usually use the word *diary* for a personal and intimate document and, therefore, that emotional tone infuses this memory of a child's life in the nursery even when that record incorporates distinct observations of the child on a regular basis.

The Purpose of the Diary

The purpose of the diary is clearly stated from the outset. Perhaps that seems a simple point, but in fact, observational methods and techniques are often employed with good intentions but in ways too vague, broad, and complicated to be really fruitful because their focus and purpose was not clearly understood and agreed upon at the start.

For Whom the Diary Is Intended

Again, the clarity of how the diary will be used and with whom it will be shared is important for the staff making the entries in the diary. This can be helpful in making sure they use language that is straightforward rather than full of technical terms that families may struggle to understand. Because its language is so direct and clear, the information gathered about Laura can be shared with the family on an ongoing basis. The parents in turn are able to add their own observations from home, which combined give a much fuller picture of how Laura's development in both contexts is progressing. This is exemplified well in the incident of "The Contested Doll," in which Laura's play at home and at the infant-toddler center can only be fully understood when sharing of observations occurs between family members and educators. In Scotland, educators often share information about the child with parents in an ongoing informal way, but they seldom record the parents' input alongside their own observations within an overall story of a child's life in the nursery. The systematic use of this technique defines the educational diary as a tool for both teachers and parents.

Recording the Diary

Who records is another area that is clearly defined. In this case, who would record was a straightforward decision, since Eluccia and Ivetta were the only two educators in the room. The assignment of two people to make observations on the same child is clearly significant in light of the fact that children's development takes place in the context of relationships, and therefore experiences can feel and be different for the child depending on which educator is supporting the child at any given time. Assigning more than one person to observe a child is best practice; when more than two people are expected to observe a child, the overall process may become time-consuming and difficult to manage, particularly when it comes to organizing and integrating the notes.

Development takes place in the context of relationships.

The Entries' Uncomplicated Nature

It can be difficult to record the significant events in a child's life and capture their developmental significance, and this may cause educators to forget the value of brevity. Laura's diary, not weighed down by words, is easy to read over and over again, each time finding new meaning.

What to Record

Laura's diary will be very helpful to educators working with very young children who are trying to decide what is a significant milestone. The word *significant* is crucial here, since educators can struggle with what exactly to record across the range of developments in a young child's life. Diary entries about Laura offer insight into what a significant milestone can look like and also provide us with really good examples of developmental steps considered in relation to one another.

The Learning Process and the Educator's Crucial Role

The learning process is vividly captured in the sequence of Laura and the watch, in which the essence of the child's discovery is encapsulated in both written and visual recordings. The educator plays a critical role by recognizing an important learning possibility, seizing upon it, and supporting Laura in developing it. This particular sequence is useful to discuss with adults working with infants, since they tend to doubt whether children can reach such an understanding in so short an interchange. Revisiting this sequence allows them to reflect upon what they know about teaching and learning and helps them to ponder young children's true capabilities.

When to Record

Laura's teachers took many more notes on Laura than are included in *Story of Laura*. Notice that the entries are dated to highlight when significant milestones were reached or significant events occurred. This document does not adhere to a systematic regime of daily entries, something the word *diary* can also imply.

Making the Child Visible

Making the child visible brings the written entry to life. Interestingly, the use of documentation through words and images to give visibility to a child's development and progress has become more usual now than it was twenty years ago. In Scotland this illuminating type of recording is used in many ways across a range of media and a variety of contexts to reveal to children, parents, and staff the ways in which children are developing and learning.

The purpose of considering these issues of observational strategy one by one is to suggest how each point of analysis can contribute to the overall understanding of the educational diary, not only as one child's story but also as a very practically based professional-development tool. The same goal is seen in the set of questions for reflection offered by Carolyn Edwards in the final chapter for those wishing to refine their observation and interpretation skills in infant-toddler settings. Such questions can be very helpful in provoking a professional dialogue and illuminating this kind of observational process, and other deeper questions will undoubtedly emerge as the dialogue to search for deeper meanings continues. Through such a process, educators will be inspired to reframe their findings and conclusions into further questions. The ongoing cycle of questioning will demonstrate that observational research has become an essential tool of best practice in early-years education and care.

Being part of supporting the development of best practice in Scotland is critically important to my current work. Reflecting on Laura's diary and its possible use for professional-development purposes has caused me to be more thoughtful and to engage in professional conversations with educators about observational and recording methods

Other deeper questions will undoubtedly emerge.

in current use. These conversations have encouraged my colleagues and me to think more deeply about how and what we observe, as well as whether observations can be used for purposes other than informing planning and staff discussions. Laura's diary helps us consider alternate perspectives on the use of observations and provokes us to build on our own understandings of our culture and pedagogical base.

An example of this kind of reflection occurred recently when I was visiting an early-years setting. In preparation for a certain child leaving the program, one of the educators was adding comments to a folder of photographs taken during the child's stay. What was clear to me was that the folder represented a deep connection between the child, the family, and the educator, yet it felt incomplete because neither the family nor the educator was visible in the folder's contents. Provoked by my recent reflections on Laura's diary, I was able to engage in a really meaningful discourse with the staff team about further possibilities for developing such a memory of the child's life in the early-years setting.

Conversations like this with staff teams, both in their settings and in professional-development courses, will continue to be developed. The publication of Laura's diary with its embedded professional-development element will be immensely helpful for us in Scotland and, I hope, in other nations as well.

✿

Pat Wharton is an early-years pedagogical consultant in Scotland. She has experience working within a wide spectrum of education, including early childhood, primary, secondary, and post-secondary education. The main emphasis of her work during the last twenty years has been in early childhood education, where she has gained international recognition for her powerful and passionate commitment to the importance of early learning. She has collaborated in preparing national documents drawing on the experience of Reggio Emilia and its implications for work in Scotland. Her new book with Linda Kinney is An Encounter with Reggio Emilia: Children's Early Learning Made Visible, *published by Routledge in 2008.*

Abbott, Lesley, and Cathy Nutbrown, eds. 2001. *Experiencing Reggio Emilia: Implications for pre-school provision.* Philadelphia: Open University Press.

Kinney, Linda, and Pat Wharton. 2007. *An encounter with Reggio Emilia: Children's early learning made visible.* London: Routledge.

LAURA'S DIARY

AN AUSTRALIAN PERSPECTIVE

Jan Millikan
Reggio Emilia Australia Information Exchange
Victoria, Australia

The images of Laura and the watch have become known worldwide, first shared by the educators in Reggio Emilia and later appearing in many publications, including the traveling exhibition "The Hundred Languages of Children." The wonderful sequence of photographs in the watch story provokes many individual interpretations, both fleeting and intense, as we try to understand what is made visible and what it could or should mean for those working with young children. The photographs not only capture precious moments in the life of one young child but also illustrate many aspects of the educational process in Reggio Emilia, including the teachers' strong belief and valuing of the rich resourceful competent child, the crucial importance of pedagogical documentation, and the relationship and reciprocity between adults and children in the process of learning and making connections.

This publication of the full *Story of Laura* has now provided the world not only with an extended image of Laura and her transition from home to infant-toddler center but also with a glimpse of the possible impact of her center experiences on her family life.

In addition, it provides a rich opportunity to consider the remarkable incident of Laura and the watch in relation to the broader range of her experiences, made visible through documentation and the collaboration of her two teachers.

There are many possible ways to interpret Laura's diary, but I wish to highlight the power of listening with the eyes, the heart, and the intellect, and the choices made about particular incidents to record. I also wish to speak about the extraordinary number, as well as the diversity, of relationships that occur in Laura's transition from home to school, and the significance of creating a safe and familiar place for children and families. This ambience of welcoming, acceptance, and warmth, so evident to the reader, seems to create a sense of belonging that deeply influences how the infant-toddler center experience influences relationships between center and home, as well as within the family.

Listen . . . with the eyes, the heart, and the intellect.

In reflecting on the various diary entries, I have considered them from an Australian perspective, where it is usual for full-day child care and education settings to include a large number of children attending on a part-time basis. Thus, on any one day, only ten children may be attending in the particular age group represented by Laura; however, the two teachers concerned could have as many as thirty children attending during the period of a week. Laura's diary heightens our awareness of the importance of time for children, teachers, and families to build relationships slowly and consistently when many children attend on a part-time basis only, and it raises questions about how to make sure these relationships are sustained both within and between groups of teachers, children, and families. The physical work alone in recording and organizing pedagogical documentation for a larger number of children provides an enormous challenge to Australians involved in full-day programs who are already undervalued in terms of wages and working conditions.

There is also a cultural dimension to building relationships, since in Australia, as in many countries of the world (including Italy in recent years), the cultural and ethnic diversity of our populations is rapidly increasing. Parents may become anxious when they have to leave a very young child in the care of others who may not be able to communicate with them verbally or in a written form. I raise these issues to further extend our thinking and sensitivity to this situation and to reflect on what could be possible. I want to challenge us to search for new opportunities for dialogue that enables us to embrace the underlying values and principles illustrated in *Story of Laura*, while at the same time improving our sensitivity to ethnic and cultural diversity and its potential for enriching the interaction of educators, families, and children.

I will consider the entries in *Story of Laura* from the perspective of transition to care in the infant-toddler center, part-time attendance, and ethnic and cultural diversity.

"Who Is Laura?"

The initial sharing and gathering of information related to Laura's birth and her early experiences of life within her family environment are the beginning of an extended relationship that will develop over the school year. The particular information sought from families may reassure them that the teachers want to understand their children's previous experiences and alleviate their concerns. The teachers can then create an individualized transition process to help each child move from an established and familiar environment (the home) toward feelings of familiarity, acceptance, and joy in the many new relationships that he or she is about to encounter in a totally new environment.

I am reminded of Malaguzzi's (1996, 47) words in the catalog of "The Hundred Languages of Children" exhibit:

> A child is born a first time, and then, through the long and difficult process of constructing his identity, it is as if he is born again. In this process, he gives himself a face, a body, gestures, movement, speech, thought, feelings, imagination, fantasy; in short, the *awareness of being* and the *means of expressing his "me-ness"* which are absolutely essential for becoming autonomous and distinguishing ourselves from other people and things—people and things we live and interact with and from which, little by little, we draw most of the raw material with which we create our own identity.

The sequence of photographs in "Who Is Laura?" could be a wonderful support for all families during the period of transition. They could provide a valuable entry point for sharing children's first experiences with families in which communication through the dominant language is not a possibility and interpreters are not readily accessible. The photos would provide a reassurance of the teacher's genuine interest and concern for the children and their learning and also act as an important catalyst for the development of relationships for these particular families.

Yet the documentation also raises time issues for teachers who have responsibility for as many as thirty children attending on a part-time basis. In such a situation, who can actually collect the information? In Australian centers, it might be necessary to involve a nonteaching director who does not have a primary caregiving assignment.

"Help from the Mobiles"

The story of Laura's transition continues with an account of her first outburst of crying as she realizes her mother, Filomena, has departed (probably to the next room). The diary tells us of the delicacy of the situation. Eluccia, the teacher, comments, "I am not sure how to calm this first cry." This indicates her awareness about the importance of her response, yet her fear that she might do the wrong thing. It is a critical moment with implications for the whole initial stage of transition. Eluccia uses the mobile to calm Laura, and Laura's positive response provides the teacher with an important tool for future interactions.

For an Australian educator, the story of the mobile raises the issue of how teachers can quickly get to know every child when they are working with a greater number of children without the consistency of daily contact and, furthermore, with the possibility that children come from a broader range of ethnic and cultural backgrounds. Our repertoire of responses may need to be broadened.

"Difficulties during Diaper Change"

The next entry highlights yet another moment in the process of transition, one that takes place during the carrying out of an everyday caregiving routine. The child brings to the diapering situation her firm expectations not only about how it should be done, but also who should be doing it (someone familiar, such as a parent). So there are two transitions occurring simultaneously, the first involving her acceptance of a new procedure for a very familiar routine, and the second involving her developing trust in a less familiar adult who is trying to make the experience acceptable. Once again, the sensitivity and empathy shown by the adult in response to Laura's distress demonstrates the importance of taking time and seeking to get in tune with Laura's own rhythms and responses.

This incident again brings up questions regarding the formation of relationships with children who are attending on a part-time basis and/or who might come from diverse family backgrounds in which alternative ways of feeding, changing, and putting babies to sleep exist. Rather than adhering rigidly to particular processes, teachers will need to become more flexible and view the relationships (not the routines) as the primary issue.

"The First Kiss to Daddy"

The ease with which Laura is able to part from her father raises many interesting questions. Does her smooth farewell occur because she already trusts the teachers? Or is it the result of her less dependent relationship with her father than with her mother? Or does it indicate that Laura is now beginning to feel more comfortable in this new place? Most of all, how can teachers interpret children's behavior when they don't know them or their family routines well?

Ivetta's surprise reminds us that each child responds in a unique way to particular situations. Nevertheless, despite not fully understanding the child's inner feelings, her welcoming interest in Laura's father, his amiable responses, and the relaxed, comfortable time they take to interact with each other all undoubtedly contribute to this moment of mutual pleasure among parent, teacher, and child. Ivetta's verbal and nonverbal communication and outreach to the family overcome any barriers to understanding. Such teacher behavior could easily translate to settings that include part-time children and those with ethnic and cultural diversity.

"The Contested Doll"

This incident marks the first time that Laura argues over a toy and also the first time that we become aware of her interacting with a peer. As an only child, Laura may have had few opportunities in her life to interact with other children; engaging with peers, as well as adults, may represent another transition for her. The teacher responds to the infants' conflict not by giving attention to either of the girls and their particular behaviors, but instead by finding an experience (pointing to the doll's eyes and nose) that provides a common endeavor and engagement.

In a setting in which children attend only on a part-time basis, they may have little opportunity to interact with the same peers. What does this mean in terms of developing close and meaningful relationships between children?

"The First Imitation Game"

This delightful entry offers insight into home experiences and suggests the importance of sharing between teachers and families in building meaningful learning environments. It opens with the teacher sharing the story of the contested doll with Laura's mother and thereby demonstrating an interest in creating dialogues with the family about Laura's learning and development. Laura's mother responds by telling about Laura's cuddling the doll at home.

When later that morning Laura uses a spoon to "feed" the doll, she may be revealing that she feels safe and comfortable, secure enough to try out a new behavior of imitative play. The incident illustrates the importance of having objects within the center that are familiar to all the children and representative of different ethnic and cultural experiences. Such familiar objects may increase the children's sense of comfort and also trigger memories that stimulate the imitation of events experienced at home.

"The Apple in the Kitchen"

This episode begins with Filomena's announcement that Laura took her first steps the previous night at home. Taking first steps is a momentous achievement for any infant and for the child's family. How pleasant it must be for parents to report their child's accomplishment and find that teachers share their joy! What might it mean for families when language barriers prevent them from sharing such an experience with the teachers, especially in the case in which no extended family or friends are near to share such a special occasion? The story highlights the importance of teachers taking time to build relationships and being ready to receive information as well as to give it.

Laura's walk to the kitchen represents a widening of Laura's relationships to include the cook and her staff, as well as a widening of her experience to include the new environment of the kitchen. This exciting experience would be denied to our young children in Australia because of strict health regulations, but I wonder what it means for toddlers to explore their entire center environment and make friends with the cook in the company of a peer. The story raises a question about part-time children, for whom the process of developing social relationships and physical knowledge of their center may be much slower than occurs for full-time children.

The Remaining Stories

Laura's explorations with the mirror and the drawer provide further illustrations of her willingness to initiate new experiences that help her develop an understanding of herself in relationship to the various resources within the center and to explore and experiment with their possibilities. What are the boundaries? What is possible? What is permissible? In these early days, the transition to new people, environments, objects, and events within the environment seems endless, and each experience yields trust of significant others as new adventures are offered. When Laura takes a small journey aboard the big stroller, waves and greetings display that she recognizes other people and considers them significant in her extended experience of life. Is the world inside and outside the center gradually becoming an increasingly safe and comfortable place?

As the diary concludes with the well-known episode of the watch, I am conscious that the rich stories of Laura took place in spite of her minimal verbal language. The observations and documentation grow out of the teachers' abilities to listen with their eyes, hearts, and intellects, and then to respond sensitively and appropriately. There also appears to be a genuine listening that allows time for Laura's own responses to be heard. Through her many languages of communication, the two-way process of developing relationships is enabled and realized in the all-important transitions to the center as well as the return transition to home.

Each experience yields trust of significant others.

Pedagogical documentation provides us with many possibilities not only for understanding and becoming close to individual children but also for interpreting how each child is influenced by interactions with teachers and other children (Fleet, Patterson, and Robertson 2006). It provides a tool for heightening our awareness of the many relationships involved in the transition to the center and how these relationships promote a sense of belonging and reciprocal knowledge of the child by the teachers and of the teachers by the child. It makes visible to the parents the depth of these relationships and also clarifies the difference between the particular relationships of child to teacher and child to parents. In this way, it completes the circle of relationships among the three protagonists (Rinaldi 2001).

The educational project in Reggio Emilia was not intended to provide a model, but we can take the opportunity to interpret the work as it is made visible to us. Documentation like Laura's diary provides us many opportunities to reflect on our own work with and for children in Australia and opens new possibilities to our minds as we become concerned with the rights of our youngest children, their teachers, and their families (Gandini and Kaminsky 2007; Millikan 2003). We deal every day with the effects of the provision of long-day programs for young children, including the resultant discontinuity of part-time attendance, but, when approached mindfully and patiently, many strategies exist for building relationships even under these circumstances. Furthermore, Australia's cultural diversity is encountered daily, but the documentation opens our minds to making sure that all differences are acknowledged and respected and that every child and family experiences a sense of belonging and value. I believe the educational diary can provide us with an important advocacy tool as we continually strive for greater recognition of the importance of the early years.

Jan Millikan is director of the Reggio Emilia Australia Information Exchange (REAIE) and an associate in the Education Faculty, Monash University, Australia. Her educational interest is strongly connected to children two to eight years of age, and she has been involved in teaching in urban and rural Victoria, the United Kingdom, Singapore, and Canada. She first visited Reggio Emilia eighteen years ago and in 1995 became Reggio Children's reference person for Australia and New Zealand. She has organized numerous study tours to Reggio and brought the traveling exhibition to Australia in 1994 and 2001. She has authored many articles, and her book Reflections: Reggio Emilia Principles within Australian Contexts *(Pademelon Press) was published in 2003.*

Fleet, Alma, Catherine Patterson, and Janet Robertson. 2006. *Insights: Behind early childhood pedagogical documentation.* Castle Hill, New South Wales: Pademelon Press.

Gandini, Lella, and Judith Allen Kaminsky. 2007. Interview with Jan Millikan, Reggio Emilia Australia Information Exchange, and Robin Duckett and Emma Pace, ReFocus Network/Sightlines Initiative, United Kingdom. *Innovations in early education: The international Reggio exchange* 14 (4).

Malaguzzi, Loris. 1996. The importance of seeing yourself again. In *The hundred languages of children: Narrative of the possible. Proposals and intuitions of children from the infant-toddler centers and preschools of the city of Reggio Emilia.* Catalog of the exhibit *The hundred languages of children.* Municipality of Reggio Emilia Infant-Toddler Centers and Preschoools. Reggio Emilia, Italy: Reggio Children.

Millikan, Jan. 2003. *Reflections: Reggio Emilia principles within Australian contexts.* Castle Hill, New South Wales: Pademelon Press.

Rinaldi, Carlina. 2001. The pedagogy of listening: The listening perspective from Reggio Emilia. *Innovations in early education: The international Reggio exchange* 8 (4).

CONTEXTUALIZING THE WATCH
EPISODE OF LAURA
ITS SIGNIFICANCE TO
KOREAN EDUCATORS

Moonja Oh
Korean Center for Children and Teachers
Seoul, Korea

When first introduced on the Korean early educational scene, the Reggio Emilia approach was often misunderstood as requiring certain procedures to follow. Even today we sometimes still strive to learn how to "do Reggio," an orientation that leads inevitably to asking exactly *how* "it" can be done here in Korea (Oh 2005). Questions such as *why* we might want to look into the Reggio experience and *what* it entails are not always raised or as vigorously discussed as they should be.

Laura's diary helps point us in a different direction. The little story of Laura and the watch first became known to Korean educators when "The Hundred Languages of Children" exhibit opened in Seoul in 2002. The watch episode was displayed on the very first panel, reflecting its high level of significance to Reggio educators. The six black-and-white images seemed to epitomize or symbolize the Reggio spirit, a force seeking to integrate educational philosophy and developmental theories with real-life observations of children, just as Carlina Rinaldi describes in her 1983 introduction to the original diary. Koreans marveled at the succinctness of the panel and the contrasting power of the message.

Indeed, the message of Laura and the watch was hard to miss and easily grasped. Once apprehended, the underlying concepts were contagious. The story of Laura became a kind of antidote for the "doing Reggio" orientation in the Korean context and helped direct our attention toward the image of the child and what it means to educate, as opposed to "doing" an educational approach.

A Story: The Episode of Laura and the Watch

The watch episode is short but rich in meaning, and it offers a supreme example of good teacher-child interaction. It elucidates the possible roles of the teacher and the child, as well as the dynamics of how their roles can change during dialogue. In addition, the episode has inherent value beyond the strictly educational because it celebrates human potential. As a story, it contains all the necessary narrative elements for capturing people's minds. In just six panels, it presents a dramatic episode with a beginning, a middle, and a conclusion that has a satisfying climax.

The episode . . . celebrates human potential.

The story shows that the child is social in nature and competent in communication. The child even anticipates the support from her teacher and knows how to solicit others' help in her own inquiry about the world. She uses all of the communicative strategies at her disposal, including looking intensely into the teacher's eyes, pointing at the photograph, and tilting her head toward the teacher. She actively strives to establish common ground with the teacher by making her message sufficiently redundant. She expresses her commitment and seriousness by changing her posture and her facial expression, most memorably, her eyebrows.

How about the teacher? The story shows a sensitive teacher supporting the child's exploration by listening and following the child's lead. At one point, she takes the initiative during the interaction and raises the ante by offering Laura the watch's tick-tock sound to widen her horizon. The teacher might at first be considered as the background for this particular event, and yet she actively establishes joint attention with Laura—the necessary step toward finding common ground and a shared framework for dialogue.

She actively strives to establish common ground.

Korean educators interpreted this episode as an example of what can happen when a sensitive adult becomes engaged with an active and inquisitive child. Overall, the watch episode succeeded in inducing Korean educators to question their images of the child as passive and incompetent, and instead consider children as competent in making connections and forming and testing hypotheses to understand their world. This message was especially persuasive due to Laura's rather "short" life history: only twelve months! The role of the sensitive adult, however, was glimpsed but not yet fully grasped. Moreover, the importance of the sustained collaborative endeavor between Laura and her teachers was neither highlighted nor appreciated at our first encounter with the diary. Laura had been at the infant-toddler center only two months when the episode occurred—seemingly an insignificant amount of time. From the perspective of the twelve-month span of her whole life, two months of new experience in the infant-toddler center would be "not so short" to Laura herself.

The power of excellent documentation led us to pose new questions, but these questions at first were still based on our old frame of mind. When the moments filled with "ahs!" and "ohs!" were over, teachers began to ask, "Where do we have to start to have wonderful episodes like those?"

Several questions immediately surfaced. First came, "How can we capture these precious moments?" Teachers seemed to believe it to be a matter of capturing critical moments in time. Soon enough, however, they realized that capturing moments required the capacity to read the conversational cues or to get the sense of the child's rhythm, and most importantly, to see what is yet to come. That insight led to another set of questions: "How do we know when to intervene or not to intervene?" "What does it mean for a teacher to be sensitive, and how can we become such a teacher?" "Are our children really as inquisitive as Laura?" And finally, "What do we have to observe and document?"

The questions posed by Korean educators in response to the watch episode seem to reveal three common themes, or pitfalls: dualism, fragmentation, and outcome orientation. We are dualistic when we put things into two separate, contrasting categories instead of seeing the connections between these categories: child's world versus adult's world, process versus product, teaching/intervening versus not teaching/not intervening, and past versus present, or present versus future. We fragment when we focus on the watch episode as though the event and its participants can be isolated from the flow of time and its surroundings. We become too outcome-oriented when we imply that the child and teacher should attain certain qualifications and work separately for the mastery of their own development. Seeking for accountability and measurable outcomes, we look for something to document rather than documenting something for reflection and dialogue. Producing beautiful documentations, such as the watch episode, becomes the ultimate goal for the teacher, rather than a means to learning about children and the teaching and learning process.

A Story with History and Context: Story of Laura

It is in this sense that *Story of Laura* has great meaning for Korean educators. Laura's diary meticulously shows that this wonderful watch episode is not just some fortunate accident that can happen whenever an inquisitive child and a sensitive teacher suddenly come together. This diary possibly can add significance to the familiar watch episode for Korean educators along two dimensions. First, it reveals the *temporal* dimension or "the time of relationship" (Edwards 2002), that is, the history of Laura building mutual trust and complex relationships up to that point. The watch episode is the result of a cumulative and still ongoing process of forming a community. Second, this diary adds another dimension to the episode, namely, the *breadth* of her relationship, highlighting Laura's ever-expanding network of relationships, including teachers, peers, children in other groups, cooks, and her own family. To sum up, the diary can make us realize that learning and development happen in the context and history of long, wide, and well-established relationships.

Unlike the traditional view of teacher-child interaction, with one party influencing the other, this diary also shows Laura and the teacher working together to create experiences in a very interdependent way. As can be seen from the episodes of "Help from the Mobiles" and "Difficulties during Diaper Change," the two teachers and the child seem to grow toward each other, rather than the child doing all of the accommodating and adjusting to the existing system, routines, and adults. The process of mutual adjustments and influences continues to go on throughout the remainder of the diary, culminating in "The Watch's Tick-Tock," as they co-construct a shared context for communication, learning, and development.

This partnership view of the teacher-child interaction offers a new way to address some perpetual concerns of Korean early childhood educators. For example, the concern for *when to intervene and when to stay out* in face-to-face interaction with children can be seen to reflect the traditional one-party direction of influence thinking, because it derives from an assumption of a clear boundary between the child's world and the teacher's world. It evokes a mental picture of the teacher standing outside the bubble in which the child resides. The partnership view, in contrast, has the potential of forcing us to rethink our perspective on the teacher-child interaction. The partnership view assumes that the teacher and the child are already participating in the experience together, as sociocultural developmental psychologist Barbara Rogoff (2003) argues, leaving no boundary to cross. The question of when to intervene and when not to becomes a false problem, and instead, the teacher can be understood to be working with the children in a series of constantly evolving, intersubjective spaces during most moments of the school day. The question then becomes *how to engage or how to co-construct* with children.

What it means . . . to be sensitive can be redefined.

In a similar vein, the issue of what it means for a teacher to be *sensitive* can be redefined. Instead of asking how the teacher should be sensitive to finding the very right moment to imbue certain facts and a body of knowledge to children, being sensitive comes to mean the teacher's willingness to adjust his or her own expectations and goals in response to the child's intentions, feelings, and desires.

We also gain new perspective on the old complaint about the lack of an *inquisitive* attitude in our children that assumes inquisitiveness is a static and fixed trait that is either present or not present in the child. The partnership view, in contrast, assumes that children dynamically learn and develop their potentials in contexts. Instead of asking a closed and backward-looking question, such as "Are our children really inquisitive?" we might want to ask ourselves, in line with the partnership view, an open and forward-looking question, such as "How do we bring out and foster inquisitiveness in our children?"

Revisit the questions of how and what to document.

Finally, *Story of Laura* can help us Korean educators revisit the questions of how and what to document. When documentation is viewed as producing evidence of learning achievements rather than making visible the learning process, creating satisfying documentation becomes almost impossible because it involves chasing something that always seems to be just over the horizon or hidden from sight. On the contrary, in the diary, ordinary simple episodes like those of Laura having a conflict with her peer in "The Contested Doll" or searching for more paper in "Discovering the Drawer" are recorded and later reflected on. These little, ordinary, everyday episodes pave the way to the rather grand hypothesis testing we see in "The Watch's Tick-Tock." In fact, that culminating episode provides a context to reinterpret the earlier ones retrospectively; we can move forward in our analysis and interpretation by looking back through the accumulated documentation. The diary makes us realize the artificiality of separating the *process* from the *product* of experiences. This realization that it isn't necessary to find a great achievement to document, but instead that we may focus on the ordinary moments, might help Korean teachers stop worrying about how and what to observe and document, and instead allow them to focus on how to find the meaning in any moments they happen to document throughout the children's day.

Redefining "Context" to Add Significance to Story of Laura

We often talk about the child learning and developing in context. Context is usually interpreted as what surrounds or envelopes the child, implying that the child is the figure while the context is the ground. If we look at its derivation, the word *context* comes from the Latin words *com*—"together"—and *textere*—"to weave." Following the etymology, we can say that the child learns and develops by weaving together an experience with others. Many discourse analysts argue that, in any interaction, participants become contexts for one another (Bloome et al. 2004). No one party is constantly determining what happens in the interaction; instead, it is a dynamic process, a transaction.

In a similar vein, we can also say that authentic dialogue generates a conversation that is interconnected and constantly evolving. In the 1930s, Russian literary critic Mikhail Bakhtin proposed the concept of *dialogicality*, arguing that any utterance or passage is always a response to some utterance or passage in the past (Bakhtin [1930s] 1981). This process of interweaving goes on endlessly, making it impossible to separate past, present, and future in any long-term interaction in a group (Forman et al. 1998).

It is now time to contextualize the old familiar story of Laura and the watch to construct a new and richer meaning. The watch episode is not a fragmented and isolated story. It is a point in an ever-evolving narrative. From this diary, we can now "see" Laura and her teachers working together in the complex web of relationships and history. The *Story of Laura* can serve as an "excuse," following Carlina Rinaldi's (2006) vision, for us Korean educators and for educators the world over to reflect again on the question of what it means to educate. To be educators demands that we be aware of and actively seek out the dynamic and multiple nature of dialogue among the children, the teachers, and the community of which they are a part. In educating children, we also need a willingness to form relationships, while honoring each child as an active and competent participant in the complex and long-term project of education.

Congratulations to Laura-then and Laura-now, who must be continuing her journey for growth within the context she herself creates along with others around her!

FURTHER READINGS

Kaminsky, Judith, and Lella Gandini. 2008. An interview with Moonja Oh. *Innovations in early education: The international Reggio exchange* 15 (1).

Oh, Moonja. 2008. Korean early childhood education and care in relation to the Reggio educational philosophy. *Innovations in early education: The international Reggio exchange* 15 (1).

Moonja Oh, EdD, is an educational consultant and teacher educator in Korea. As the director of the Korean Center for Children and Teachers (KCCT), she conducts seminars and workshops for pre-school and kindergarten teachers and also lectures at various graduate schools in Seoul. Since her first visit to Reggio Emilia in 1994, she has been working with Korean children and classroom teachers to infuse the spirit of Reggio Emilia education, on the basis of which she has written a book (in Korean), Reggio Emilia and Our Children. She currently serves as the president of the Korean Association for the Reggio Emilia Approach (KAREA), and she has organized several study tours to Reggio Emilia and international conferences and has helped to bring "The Hundred Languages of Children" exhibit to her country.

Bakhtin, Mikhail M. [1930s] 1981. *The dialogic imagination: Four essays*, ed. Michael Holquist and Vadim Liapunov. Trans. Caryl Emerson and Michael Holquist. Austin and London: University of Texas Press.

Bloome, David, Stephanie P. Carter, Beth M. Christian, Stella Otto, and Nora Shuart-Faris. 2004. *Discourse analysis and the study of classroom language and literacy events: A microethnographic perspective*. Mahwah, NJ: Laurence Erlbaum Associates.

Edwards, Carolyn P. 2002. Participation and community: What is "education as relationship" in early childhood education? Presented at the "Educare as Partnership" conference, June 7–8, ChungAng University, Seoul, Korea.

Forman, George, Joan Langley, Moonja Oh, and Lynda Wrisley. 1998. The city in the snow: Applying the multisymbolic approach in Massachusetts. In *The hundred languages of children: The Reggio Emilia approach, advanced reflections*. 2nd ed. Carolyn Edwards, Lella Gandini, and George Forman, eds. Greenwich, CT: Ablex.

Oh, Moonja. 2005. Opening address: Searching for the future direction of the Korean Association for the Reggio Emilia Approach (KAREA). Presented at the KAREA conference, "Celebrating Diversity," July 2–3, Seoul, Korea.

Rinaldi, Carlina. 2006. *In dialogue with Reggio Emilia: Listening, researching and learning*. London and New York: Routledge.

Rogoff, Barbara. 2003. The *cultural nature of human development*. New York: Oxford University Press.

"TELL LAURA I LOVE HER, TELL LAURA I NEED HER"

A SWEDISH SONG

Harold Göthson
Reggio Emilia Institute
Stockholm, Sweden

These lyrics from a song popular with teenagers in my youth came into my mind when I once again met the educational *Story of Laura*. We need stories like this; we need testimonies of a new and strong message of children's potentials and rights. We need them to combat the images of children as poor and needy that so readily dominate our pedagogical minds, actions, and traditions. We need them so we can confront these dominating discourses within ourselves and our scientific and everyday lived cultures. We need them to create a new educational culture that depends on multiple interpretations. We need Laura's diary for its openness, as opposed to a closed version of the "real truth." The greatness of Laura's story is the way it offers a responsible and visible choice of perspectives that can support and give Laura (and all children) a sense of being a gift to humankind. It's a story of welcoming.

Thinking about this draws us toward love in the Greek concept of *agape*, the love connected to all human beings, to life in its astonishing appearance in everyone. In the English language, lovers express their appreciation of each other by saying, "You make the difference," words easy to express in the beginning of a relationship but often reduced to ambitions to make the other like the self when we try to share our lives together. Instead, we should appreciate the differences and challenges of the other in a mutual journey of discovery. We need tools for confirming the other as the other and not the same, tools such as Laura's story that help us experience and together construct a meaning of the concept of love as a matter of reciprocal interdependence.

Discover, create, and confirm the appreciation of childhood.

From our creating of stories confirming our love, we need to go on telling this story to all children, including Laura, and to each other and the world. We should tell our children about our appreciation and our wish to let them astonish us and fill us with amazement. Pedagogical documentation is built on the wish to discover, create, and confirm the appreciation of childhood and the contributions of children. In that way, it fosters a culture of listening and mutual understanding with respect for differences, and in fact, creates and redefines what we mean by *democracy*. Then documentations and stories can turn into real moments of democracy, as Carlina Rinaldi (2001) once formulated it. So again, tell Laura I love her, tell Laura I need her.

To Meet Something That Makes You Reflect

Writing this essay has given me an opportunity to reflect once again upon the Swedish inspiration from Reggio Emilia, as well as upon my own process of formulating an educational philosophy. The writing became a tool and reason for reflection. I would call this a metastructure for learning, to be invited into a situation that makes it possible to listen to your own thoughts and actions and in which you can experiment and try to find conclusions, create hypotheses, and perhaps give meaning to your experience. This was for me a situation of meeting and listening to "the other," in this case Laura's diary, in which I could use and formulate my experience and could express and expand my capacity to give meaning to a question. Intelligence was required; our late friend, Loris Malaguzzi, used to speak of the situation, "A ball is thrown that makes me wish to go on playing the game."

Becoming an Individual Identity in Intelligent Relations

Laura's story may be understood at first as the brilliance of one human being. In our initial interactions, Swedish educators felt awe when confronted by the images of children in Reggio Emilia. It was a reaction connected to the following thought: this is special, and we do not have such children in our context. Overwhelmed, we sought a defensive strategy. The challenge of the watch story is to see Laura as "every child," and then make the ethical choice to meet every child as intelligent. This puts a critical eye on how well the schools and educators support and make sensible each child's capacity.

This makes me reflect on the situation in which Laura's diary was created, the intelligent situation of welcoming that focuses not only on Laura as an individual but also as a participant in a system of relations in which she can become a co-player. We must expand individuality to include the concepts of intersubjectivity, reciprocity, and sharing, as well as those of being a part, involved, and engaged.

This reminds me of a dialogue that took place between five-year-old children and their teacher at the end of their preschool journey, cited in the book *Making Learning*

Visible (Project Zero and Reggio Children 2001, 323). Athina says, "When you agree on something, you can do something that's even nicer," and Anna, another child, adds, "Because your brain works better. Because your ideas, when you say them out loud, they keep coming together, and when all the ideas come together you get a gigantic idea! You can think better in a group." Such group experiences may be similar to those of Laura from the welcoming opening weeks in the infant-toddler center to the end, years later, of her time in the Anna Frank Preschool.

One strong message in *Story of Laura* is that of being involved with others in discovering and challenging her understanding of the world. It is a story of interdependence, sharing, and our capacity to move from one intelligence to another during the weeks in an infant center. Mostly it tells us that we have a potential within each of our intellects to enrich our knowledge and subjectivity by receiving and listening to other persons. The story is a message that the listening and mutual expectations that make communication possible are capacities belonging to the very small child. These social capacities belong to our species and don't need to be taught. But this leaves us with the necessary comment that the teacher in this situation is not merely extraneous. Teachers work closely with Laura to make the learning process appear between them.

One common interpretation of the books and publications from Reggio Emilia is that the teacher is rather passive and invisible and only the strength of the children is stressed. This interpretation misses the point of the quality of interaction between child and educator and shows we are still stuck in old dominant discourses in which young children are seen as pure Nature rather than socialized identities (Dahlberg 1985, 1999). Instead, we should look to the meaning of relationships and the group as a possible carrier of each individual. This is necessary to emphasize in the Swedish context in which the focus on individual learning styles tends to separate children from one another instead of inviting them to share their diversity. My fear is that the stress on learning styles leads not to the support of sharing and group projects but instead to the development of more diagnostic strategies that put children into closed definitions of their identities.

In this time of increasing globalization, we need to challenge closed definitions of identities. We need to look upon identity as plastic and a place for change and multiplicity. Laura's diary invites us into an infant-toddler center that lets her challenge and expand her image of herself and her world in relation to others.

Why Is Laura in an Infant-Toddler Center? A Tool for a New Kind of Citizenship?

How can a person become interested in something that hasn't been experienced yet? It probably comes about by being listened to, welcomed, accepted, and appreciated, as well as by being given the right to experiment with definitions of the surrounding world. Laura's world contains watches and images of watches. She becomes comfortable in finding and using her capacities and is supported in her experience of becoming secure in a world that is expanding, and that is only temporarily understood. Still, how is it possible for the child to become interested in something outside her own experience? We have to consider why this situation occurs and is offered to Laura. She finds herself in a situation in which learning is valued and made visible, in which learning is not seen as moving from superficial or incorrect understanding to higher or right understanding, but instead as a matter of expanding perspectives. This brings

Challenge closed definitions of identities.

us to other questions: Why is Laura in the infant-toddler center? What is the task of infant-toddler centers and why do we need them? What kind of tools are they for society? What values do or should they support? To what is Laura invited? What should be the nature of the welcoming? To these questions our friends in Reggio Emilia give an answer by telling the story of Laura's first weeks in her new center.

The answer that we in Sweden can share with our Reggio Emilia friends, without copying their method, is related to their choice of values. These values include subjectivity, diversity, interdependence, and learning, complemented by others, such as humor, feelings, and others that Rinaldi (2001) formulates in her essay in *Making Learning Visible*. These values are connected to an idea of school as a political and cultural tool for a new citizenship, a global democratic citizenship. Considering the school as a meeting place for families sharing their diversities challenges the older concept of Swedish preschools as similar to homes.

Yet we also have in our Swedish educational tradition, going back to the 1930s, interest in the concept of schools as first and foremost a place for fostering democracy. This concept was influenced by John Dewey's concept of "learning by doing" ([1916] 1944). Indeed, Sweden is often considered to be the most Dewey-inspired country in the world with respect to educational policies. The paradox is that this concept has been applied as a top-down project, rather than a simultaneous top-down and bottom-up project. Sometimes we say that Sweden has been child oriented in defending the rights of children through family policies and the welfare state. Loris Malaguzzi often celebrated this aspect of Swedish society, but in his visits to our country he questioned the underlying concept of child orientation. What is the image of the child and of childhood? He asked us if we didn't assume a poor and needy child, rather than a strong and competent child, as the starting point for our societal efforts at child welfare.

The Swedish Encounter with Reggio Emilia's Images of Children

The first time I encountered *Story of Laura* was when Carlina Rinaldi passionately presented the images of Laura to a group of Swedes visiting Reggio Emilia. It was an amazing introduction to the image of children that our colleagues in Reggio Emilia wished to put forward as a matter of choice guiding their organization. Laura's diary is not only a testimony to a strong and competent image of the child but also an image of knowledge and learning, and an image of what a school can be in a democracy. All these standpoints are necessary to define an educational philosophy, as has become obvious in our Swedish context of interpretation of the experience and accounts from Reggio Emilia. Our visitors have been struck by what we have seen and heard, and in the beginning, many tried to escape a bad feeling of comparison by saying that we in Sweden have the same image of the child, but the Reggio Emilia teachers are just better in their documentation, or sometimes by blaming colleagues and the leadership in Sweden for not being open to this image that many felt they shared with Reggio Emilia.

When we started to look at the encounters with Reggio Emilia as a confrontation not of sameness but of diversity, we managed to find more strength in the meetings. A good help in this step was the contribution by Gunilla Dahlberg (1985; Dahlberg, Moss, and Pence 1999) in her writings on images of children and learning. She confirmed that on the surface it could seem as though the Swedish educational context in both early childhood policies and practices was child oriented in the same way as Reggio Emilia's educational context. She also stressed that our late friend Loris Malaguzzi often celebrated the Scandinavian countries in his speeches after his visits. But having said this, she asked what we mean by child orientation in a deeper sense. Through this question it was possible to both confirm our child orientation and problematize different orientations to images of children and learning.

In her first efforts to construct new questions, Gunilla pointed to a Swedish preschool tradition dominated by an image of the child as Nature (Dahlberg 1999). This could be defined mostly within the boundaries of developmental psychology, with its focus on normal patterns of development, and is connected with a belief in concepts of free play in which the child expresses inner possibilities and constraints. In early childhood, everything is seen as within the child, and the pedagogical effort should be a careful nourishment.

This traditional view of the preschool child contrasts with what happens at the primary school, where teachers look upon the task and the child as a matter of educational and cultural reproduction, often tending to the view of child as *tabula rasa* (blank slate). Trying to reconcile these two opposites, Gunilla suggested that beyond both traditions lay a third possibility—referring to Reggio Emilia—with the image of the child and teacher as a matter of co-construction of knowledge and culture involving children, teachers, and families. Could this third possibility in fact open up a new cooperation between preschools and primary schools?

Everything is seen as within the child.

When we introduced this discourse in our networks, many new things became visible, more was able to be shared, exchanged, and reflected upon. One outcome was the awareness of recognizing our own tradition and what governed our actions and thoughts in educational work with children. Suddenly we could go on a journey of discovery, not primarily of Reggio Emilia, but instead, by using the prism they provided to us, we could describe and confront the Swedish context. This was a new way of looking at the value of sharing experiences and networking, not as a matter of mastery and making comparisons, but rather of finding mutual understanding and new meanings of ourselves and others. Instead of the destructive idea of being wrong, it became a matter of respect for ourselves as well as a tool to discover what we had taken for granted. We could welcome our history and our earlier thoughts and actions, our dominant discourses, as something to use and challenge in our understanding of our everyday life with children and parents.

Reggio Emilia had made us more interested in how we in our society look upon children, childhood, learning, and the task of schools. The meeting had made us curious about how our own society expresses itself, through teachers and schools among other ways, and at cultural, aesthetic, social, and political levels. The meeting with Reggio Emilia created a wish, not to become the same, but instead to enter into dialogue about one another's differences, becoming more aware of our own challenges and choices to develop from our contextual and historical circumstances. Therefore, we didn't choose to talk about the Reggio Emilia *approach* but rather about the Reggio Emilia *inspiration*, and today we ask ourselves if a still better formulation would not have been *in dialogue* with Reggio Emilia. The idea of knowledge connected to networks of relationships, using the metaphor of a web, was an early orientation in the founding of the Reggio Emilia Institutet in Stockholm in 1992, where I was senior director and chair for many years. After more than fifteen years in existence, we now can see the networking inspired by Reggio Emilia promoting almost a new social movement. This movement features a mostly bottom-up hope for change in early education that includes ever more

The meeting with Reggio Emilia created a wish.

educators, who then engage and involve the administrators and policy makers.

Ever since my colleague and pedagogical consultant at the Reggio Emilia Institutet, Anna Barsotti, encountered Reggio Emilia in the late 1970s and made it possible for other Swedes to relate Reggio Emilia pedagogy and practices to their own experiences, many thousands of educators from Sweden have visited Reggio Emilia (Göthson and Dahlberg 1999). Nevertheless, in 1992 when we opened our Reggio Emilia Institutet in Stockholm, we were careful to try to find new strategies to look upon children in our own context, not bringing too much focus on the work in Reggio Emilia. Mostly we have been in dialogue with their experience through yearly courses led by Vea Vecchi (Morrow 1999), and in later years through more and more meetings with Carlina Rinaldi, Amelia Gambetti, and others from Reggio Emilia. On June 14–16, 2007, we welcomed to Sweden a group of thirty experienced and younger educators, policy makers, and parents from Reggio Emilia visiting our country to look for "Reggio outside Reggio." This was a wonderful invitation to celebrate our long and mutual cooperation, and we had the honor of hosting the first meeting held outside Reggio Emilia for the worldwide network connected to the Loris Malaguzzi International Center. The center, you may know, opened in 2006 and is intended to be a space for the international community to advocate for children's rights, identity, and potential. Now all of us share the challenge of becoming partners in developing this center so that in the future we can sit together—Swedish and Nordic educators with colleagues from Reggio Emilia and many other countries of the world—sharing work based not only in Reggio Emilia but also on mutual research projects that involve many other countries.

Until now our institute has been focusing on projects with primary schools and

Try to find new strategies to look upon children.

on such topics as transculturality and children as symbol creators. Going forward, we have decided instead to give priority to studying the topic chosen for the new *ateliers* (studios) at the Loris Malaguzzi International Center: the topic of *light*. Our dream is that by choosing a similar topic also in Sweden, we shall create meeting points for sharing our different discoveries at the center and using our diversities to expand our understanding of children's relationships to the concept and phenomenon of light. In our educational networks, we have tried mostly to challenge our interpretations of our own observations and to take first steps to give meaning to pedagogical documentation. We have created a context in which it seems to be easier today than it used to be to bring stories like Laura's diary into our web of reflections. As a matter of fact, today we feel more confident to expand our networking into more meetings with other contexts beyond Reggio Emilia. Indeed, it was for this reason that I welcomed the wonderful invitation of commenting on *Story of Laura*, and I hope to find many more initiatives for educators from all countries to meet over the years to come.

The Immediate Challenges of Story of Laura in Sweden

Ending these comments I want to share some of the challenges that we are struggling with at this moment in Sweden that are provoked by *Story of Laura*.

The first challenge is finding the starting point for observing children. An attitude of curiosity and amazement is necessary to avoid objectifying the children's learning. I believe this is the first crucial point for me and for all of us: finding the belief in and amazement toward all children.

The second issue with which we struggle is deepening our understanding of documentation. We want to use it as a tool within the process and not as a comment afterwards—that is, as a tool not only for educators and families but primarily for the children's participation in their own learning processes together with educators and others. This cries for documentation that is open, not finalized. It cries for visibility that is not mainly watching but instead mostly listening, so that learning becomes something that can be shared and exchanged and a cause for celebration that we are interdependent in our learning.

The third challenge we face is our need to upgrade the value of preschools in society, both as learning communities and perhaps even more as places of daily living, where small events and episodes can be appreciated as a dialectical energy in our projecting, our flexible planning that concerns any aspect of the life of the school (Rinaldi 1998). We still struggle to find the interaction between long-term projects (big learning events) and the ordinary, everyday experiences in all children's lives. I would encourage all educators to create individual child portfolios that stress the individual as part of a system and development in relationship to others.

These thoughts reflect some of what Laura's diary will bring into my exchanges with educators, parents, and policy makers. I would like to conclude with the story of one teacher, Monica Jansson. It is a story of celebration of children's amazing strategies for reflection and communication—a small story that took place within a larger project during autumn 2005 and spring 2006, when five-year-olds at Ankaret Preschool in Kärrtorp, Sweden, worked on a project about earthworms outdoors and indoors. The children asked, "Do blue worms exist?" I think this story captures the essence of many things I have been trying to say in this essay.

"October 2: The Apple in the Kitchen"

- *What do you appreciate about this story of the visit to the kitchen?*
- *Why does teacher Eluccia leave the children in the kitchen with the cook? (Is it a curriculum decision?)*
- *Is Laura fully adjusted yet?*

"October 9: Laura and the Mirror"

- *Has Laura recognized herself or not?*
- *What might teacher Ivetta and mother talk about together regarding this episode?*

"October 12: Discovering the Drawer"

- *Why do you think Laura enjoyed the emptying game more than playing with the huge piece of paper she pulled out?*
- *Why did she return a second time to look in the original drawer, after checking in the lower drawer? (Hint: take a look at Swiss psychologist Jean Piaget's stages of the development of object permanence.)*

"October 13: On Board the Big Stroller"

- *What does this story of the ride in the big stroller say about life at the infant-toddler center?*
- *What does it say about Laura's adjustment?*

"October 21: The Watch's Tick-Tock"

- *Why might the authors of Laura's diary have chosen this particular incident to end the story of Laura's first days at the center?*

- *What was Laura thinking in each step of this story? (Can you "read" the photos?)*

- *This is an example of powerful learning. Why did it happen? What was the teacher's role?*

- *By the time of the "Tick-Tock" incident, many other things had happened. How had they established the context for this beautiful incident to take place?*

- *Is Laura fully "adjusted" now? What does adjustment have to do with the child's potential for learning at the infant-toddler center?*

- *What have you concluded about the whole process of adjustment and transition during Laura's first two months in the infant-toddler center?*

Reflections from around the World

The ways that Laura's diary resonates with readers around the world is surely remarkable and confirms that this book has the makings of an educational classic. I hope that readers will ponder and discuss the reflection questions to extract their meanings. Here follows my view of a few of the practical and realistic suggestions that are embedded in the essays, organized in lists in hopes that some teachers will find that useful.

Learn to Be a Participant Observer

A teacher is a busy person with many responsibilities. This book urges teachers to be selective and observe on the fly, to be subjective and interpretive in their note taking, and to focus on recording things that one needs to know about. But learning to be such a participant observer may seem to conflict with the type of observation training that teachers learn in college and with the types of outcome-oriented assessments required by many schools and centers. What to do? In "How the Infant Teacher's Context

Influences the Content of Diaries," Ronald Lally suggests that a new orientation to the observation process may:

~ Help teachers develop plans to assist children engage their topics of interest.

~ Convey to them a deep sense of respect and worthiness.

Use This Book as a Model of How to Do an Educational Diary

There is no single right way to do an educational diary, but the ways in which this diary is laid out provide one helpful model for teachers to consider as they seek to document the learning process of the very young child. For example, consider the following points made by Pat Wharton in "In the Footsteps of Laura's Teachers: A Scottish Perspective":

~ This diary begins with an introduction to Laura and her family that describes a few simple facts about the child's family background and what her parents hope for her to gain from her experience at the infant-toddler center.

~ It lays out its purpose for teachers as a tool for understanding the child's adjustment, for parents as a way of understanding their child from a new perspective, and for the child as a way to see herself as a subject of the teachers' love.

~ It demonstrates how two teachers can coordinate their separate observations of the child to create a unified picture.

~ It shows how short entries, written in everyday, accessible language, can convey so much in an indirect, suggestive way.

~ It takes us from an external view of the learning process to go inside the meaning of it for the child, revealing how the learning unfolds.

Operate within the Constraints of Your Situation

All teachers operate in contexts that offer many opportunities as well as some limitations. Instead of saying, "I couldn't do a diary like that. I don't have the (time/resources/support/skills)," any teacher can devise some creative solutions. For example, many teachers work in settings like those described in "Laura's Diary: An Australian Perspective" by Jan Millikan, which include a large number of children from culturally diverse backgrounds, often attending on a part-time basis. The teacher might do the following:

~ Take plenty of time to build relationships with each child and family even if this takes longer than it does when children attend on a more consistent basis.

~ Find help in collecting the information, for instance, from a nonteaching director who does not have a primary caregiving assignment.

~ Take care to find out the ways in which the families do the daily nurturing tasks of feeding, changing, and putting their babies to sleep, always viewing the relationships (not the routines) as the primary issue.

~ Use both verbal and nonverbal communication to reach out to families and convey feelings of welcoming and inclusion.

~ Bring familiar objects into the center to increase children's sense of comfort and trigger memories connected to experiences at home.

~ Be ready to receive information as well as give it.

Break Out of Unproductive Thought Patterns

Teachers, like anyone else, can fall into thinking pitfalls, according to Moonja Oh in "Contextualizing the Watch Episode of Laura: Its Significance to Korean Educators":

~ One pitfall is the tendency to think in black-and-white categories and create false dichotomies, such as child's world versus adult's world, process versus product, intervening versus not intervening, and even the time categories of past, present, and future. Rigid categories stand in the way of flexible thinking and of taking risks by questioning old assumptions, finding new connections, and being able to tolerate some ambiguity and uncertainty.

~ A second pitfall is fragmenting or isolating an event and its participants from the flow of time. Close attention to context leads to insight in making interpretations.

~ A third pitfall is to become too outcome- and achievement-oriented in seeking to produce admirable or beautiful documentation. More satisfying results come from simply letting go of judgments and documenting everyday events as a means to better understanding children and the teaching/learning process.

Find Your Strengths Within

It is all too easy to feel inferior in the face of the beautiful images from *Story of Laura* and wonder why one's own classroom isn't full of such superb documentations of learning moments. This defensive reaction is described by Harold Göthson in his essay, "Tell Laura I Love Her, Tell Laura I Need Her: A Swedish Song," and he says it generates a sense of inferiority that actually holds us back from respecting ourselves and entering into true dialogue with others. Instead, he suggests we think about the following:

~ Listen to the wisdom of teachers from every country, and grow through sharing all of our diverse interpretations.

~ Draw on Laura's diary as an example of excellent documentation, but don't rely on it as a model to follow exactly.

~ Gather with a group of teaching partners for deep conversations, and search for the strengths that come from your own background, community, local history, and special traditions.

~ Remember that every society has its own problems to solve, and every setting has its own brilliant children and precious moments waiting to be made visible. As *Story of Laura* tells us, it is a matter of love and the power of listening with the eyes, the heart, and the mind.

Make a Commitment to Relationship-Based Care for Infants and Toddlers

Relationship-based care is becoming recognized as the standard of practice in the field of early care and education (Butterfield, Martin, and Prairie 2004). It begins with the assumption that young children form affectional bonds, or attachments, with a small circle of people with whom they spend the most time (Josselson 1995). These attachments are crucial for healthy growth and development, because they create a sense of trust, security, and positive expectations in the children and support their exploration of the world. Secure attachments to primary caregivers (usually parents) and secondary caregivers (such as grandparents, older siblings, and child care providers) are fostered by an interaction style that is sensitive, consistent, warm, and appropriately responsive to each child's needs and cues. Secondary attachments support and complement, rather than detract or take away from, primary attachments, and they become "bridges" that help the child become embedded in a wider network that extends outward from the home into the neighborhood and community.

Building and protecting strong positive relationships that continue over time, therefore, is the necessary foundation for educational and intervention work with the very young child. As Greenspan and Weider (1997, 5) put it, "The child's interactions in relationships and family patterns are the primary vehicle for mobilizing development and growth." Educators, like family members, promote the infant's attachment and security when they provide contact comfort through touching, stroking, rocking, and holding; quick and appropriate responses to the child's cries and signals; support in times of distress or illness; and joy and delight in the child's antics, explorations, and desires to share and to play. Their responsive care and guidance leads children to engage in more and higher levels of physical and object play, to be more curious and exploratory in the environment, and to form close peer relationships (Honig 2002).

Attachment principles in early education and intervention programs apply not only between adults and children but also among adults and include strategies of parent-professional communication, hiring of new personnel, and supervision and in-service training (Baker and Manfredi/Petitt 2004). Both professionals and parents need to be treated (and to treat each other) as whole, developing human beings and to work as partners in supporting the children who are their common interest (Keyser 2006). For example, as teachers plan for each day and each child, they devise activities that build on each child's emerging interests, habits, talents, and capabilities, and they share their plans frequently with parents. Administrators set the organizational tone by employing hiring criteria that prioritize emotional qualities, such as rapport drive, ability to see children as individuals, warmth, and compassion. Administrators also promote staff retention through good wage structure, high morale, and a supervision process that values personal and professional growth.

American and Italian research and experience converge on a set of principles for applying the science of relationships to educational planning and decision making (adapted from Edwards and Raikes 2002). All of them were present at Arcobaleno Infant-Toddler Center.

~ Build the program around relationships and seek to support and strengthen child-parent (and peer-peer) attachments. Bring the relationship lens to all program decisions. Use relationship goals as the language for dialogue with families, colleagues, and the public.

~ Appreciate that child development takes place in family, cultural, linguistic, and historical context. Develop sensitivity and understanding for differing values, beliefs, and expectations. Nourish a sense of belonging with the local community, past and present.

~ Establish an emotionally and physically safe environment that makes children feel comfortable, protected, and looked after in a familiar place that invites them to explore, investigate, and try new challenges. As part of establishing this secure backdrop for children, implement routines and schedules that provide order and predictability to children's day.

~ Create an environment that encourages a sense of belonging to a group. Make the spaces and activities conducive to imagination, fantasy, and expression, and allow the group of children to develop their own games and rituals that create emotional connections to one another and the setting.

~ Plan curriculum around the interests and emerging skills of the children. Use methods of observation, documentation, and planning that promote interactions geared to each child's unique needs.

~ Support each child through daily separations, reunions, and moments of transition. Be aware of the caregiver's role as secure base in cushioning these change points for children.

~ Foster close relationships and dialogue with families and encourage frequent conferences, visits, and information exchange. Use empathy, emotional responsiveness, and good nonverbal communication in interactions with children and families.

~ Devote attention to introducing and orienting new children and families in a delicate, slowed down, unhurried way. Provide support for children who leave the program or move from one group to another, and try to move children together with close or familiar peers.

~ Act on the insight that children form attachments to multiple adults to help them develop and feel part of a loving world. Remember that attachments take infants and toddlers a long time to develop and are emotionally costly and time consuming to replace. Promote continuity of care, for example, by supporting "family groups" of teacher(s) and children who remain together for a prolonged, multiyear time, or by providing each child with a primary caregiver.

~ Hire staff who believe in the importance of relationships, have strong rapport, empathy, and communication skills, and are able to invest in children and families.

~ Make staff feel part of a supportive system. Think of staff development as a process, not an outcome, and attend to the emotional components of adult development during training and supervision.

~ Reduce teacher turnover through a good wage structure and make clear the program structure and the importance of commitment to continuity of care throughout the infant and toddler years.

In sum, *Story of Laura* is a simple little story, but it conveys a whole philosophy of early childhood education. It specifically tells a story about *relationships* (what Carlina Rinaldi in the opening pages of the original diary describes as events that are *between* the child and educator, child and other children, and child and the physical world). It also illustrates the potential of an educational diary and how the documentation process serves children, parents, educators, and the public. The diary tells a narrative about a child's and family's experience of the first days in the center and of a gradual, unfolding adjustment process, but each page within the booklet also tells its own ministory, and can be studied in its own right. More than twenty years later, with Laura now grown up and a thriving young adult, we feel it is a special gift to experience something so evocative as this educational diary. This narrative both stimulates emotion and sparks thought, and by right should become a classic study in the field of education.

Baker, Amy C., and Lynn A. Manfredi/Petitt. 2004. *Relationships, the heart of quality care: Creating community among adults in early care settings.* Washington, DC: National Association for the Education of Young Children.

Butterfield, Perry A., Carole A. Martin, and Arleen Pratt Prairie. 2004. *Emotional connections: How relationships guide early learning.* Washington, DC: Zero to Three Press.

Edwards, Carolyn, Lella Gandini, and George Forman, eds. 1998. *The hundred languages of children: The Reggio Emilia approach, advanced reflections.* 2nd ed. Greenwich, CT: Ablex.

Edwards, Carolyn P., and Helen Raikes. 2002. Extending the dance: Relationship-based approaches to infant/toddler care and education. *Young Children* 57 (4): 10–17.

Gandini, Lella. 2001. Reggio Emilia: Experiencing life in an infant-toddler center. Interview with Cristina Bondavalli. In *Bambini: The Italian approach to infant/toddler care.* Lella Gandini and Carolyn Edwards, eds. New York: Teachers College Press.

Gandini, Lella, and Carolyn Edwards, eds. 2001. *Bambini: The Italian approach to infant/toddler care.* New York: Teachers College Press.

Greenspan, Stanley I., and Serena Wieder. 1997. An integrated developmental approach to interventions for young children with severe difficulties in relating and communicating. *Zero to Three* 17 (5): 5–18.

Honig, Alice S. 2002. *Secure relationships: Nurturing infant-toddler attachment in early care settings.* Washington, DC: National Association for the Education of Young Children.

Josselson, Ruthellen. 1995. *The space between us: Exploring the dimensions of human relationships.* Thousand Oaks, CA: Sage Publications.

Keyser, Janis. 2006. *From parents to partners: Building a family-centered early childhood program.* St. Paul, MN: Redleaf Press.

Reggio Children. 1999. *The municipal infant-toddler centers and preschools of Reggio Emilia: Historical notes and general information.* Reggio Emilia, Italy: Reggio Children and Municipality of Reggio Emilia.

Rinaldi, Carlina. 2001. Reggio Emilia: The image of the child and the child's environment as a fundamental principle. In *Bambini: The Italian approach to infant/toddler care.* Lella Gandini and Carolyn Edwards, eds. New York: Teachers College Press.

PHOTO CREDITS

Front Cover

Photos courtesy of Arcobaleno Infant-Toddler Center and Archives of the Documentation and Educational Research Center–Preschools and Infant-Toddler Centers, Istituzione of the Municipality of Reggio Emilia.

"Introduction: Setting the Scene"

Photos on pages 2, 3, 4 (upper-left corner), and 5 (upper-right corner) courtesy of Carolyn Edwards.

Photos on pages 4 (lower-right corner) and 5 (lower-left corner) courtesy of Arcobaleno Infant-Toddler Center and Archives of the Documentation and Educational Research Center–Preschools and Infant-Toddler Centers, Istituzione of the Municipality of Reggio Emilia.

"Story of Laura"

Photos courtesy of Arcobaleno Infant-Toddler Center and Archives of the Documentation and Educational Research Center–Preschools and Infant-Toddler Centers, Istituzione of the Municipality of Reggio Emilia.

"An Encounter with Laura"

Photos courtesy of Arcobaleno Infant-Toddler Center and Archives of the Documentation and Educational Research Center–Preschools and Infant-Toddler Centers, Istituzione of the Municipality of Reggio Emilia.

"Tell Laura I Love Her, Tell Laura I Need Her: A Swedish Song"

Photos courtesy of Christina Dackeus from the municipal nurseries of Skarpnäck, Sweden.